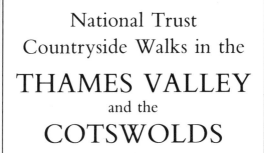

National Trust
Countryside Walks in the

THAMES VALLEY
and the
COTSWOLDS

Edited by Steve Parker

Photography by Colin Molyneux

TRAVELLERS PRESS

Contents

First published in 1985 by
Travellers Press
59 Grosvenor Street,
London W1

ISBN 1 85150 002 2

Printed in Hong Kong

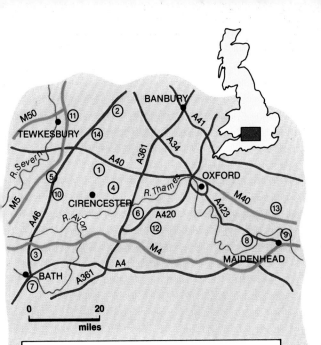

Key to Walk Map Symbols

y/m/a/f	Yards, miles, acres, feet	⊢⊢⊢⊢⊢⊢	Railway
✳	Starting point	∿	River or canal
P	Parking/car park	∽	Minor river/stream
i	Information office	====	Waterfall
T	Toilets	⋈	Bridge
✗	Picnic site		Sea or lake
V	Viewpoint		Sand or beach
⌐	Seat	♠♠♠	Woodland
→	Direction of route	◉	Individual tree
⇘	Alternative routes	ⱴⱴⱴ	Heathland
-----	Route for walkers		Parkland or green
—	Route for disabled	▲▲▲	Rocks
	Motorway	○	Cave
	All other roads	●	Gravel pit
➡	One-way traffic	ⱴⱴⱴ	Marsh or bog
	Ancient way	○	Spring
---	Long-distance path	▬	Building
-----	Footpath or track	✝	Church or chapel
⟫⟫⟩	Steep descent/ascent	✕	Cross
⚏	Steps	∧	Burial mound
▲	Dangerous path	▲	Memorial
∞∞∞	Wall	△	Youth hostel
⚡	Electric fence	▲	Trigonometric point

Walk Selector

		☐ Easy ☐ Moderate ☐ Difficult	Length (miles)	Time (hours)
Number	Name			
1★	**Chedworth**		$3\frac{1}{4}$	2
2★	**Chipping Campden**		4	2
3★	**Dyrham Park**		$5\frac{1}{2}$	3
4	**Bibury & Coln Valley**		$5\frac{1}{2}$	3
5	**Haresfield Beacon**		6	3
6	**Badbury & Coleshill**		$6\frac{1}{4}$	$3\frac{1}{2}$
7	**Bath**		$6\frac{1}{2}$	$3\frac{1}{2}$
8	**Henley & Greys Court**		7	$3\frac{1}{2}$
9	**Cookham**		7	$3\frac{1}{2}$
10	**Rodborough**		$7\frac{1}{2}$	4
11	**Bredon**		$8\frac{1}{2}$	$4\frac{1}{2}$
12★	**White Horse Hill**		9	$4\frac{1}{2}$
13	**Hughenden**		9	$4\frac{1}{2}$
14★	**Hailes Abbey**		15	$7\frac{1}{2}$

* Facilities for disabled people. Fees payable at most car parks (NT parking free for NT members)

Start/finish P Car park	Grid ref	OS map 1:50,000	OS map 1:25,000
Chedworth Villa Woodland P	SP 053 134	163	SP 01/11
Chipping Campden P	SP 151 391	150/151	SP 03/13
Dyrham House P	ST 742 757	172	ST 67/77
Bibury village (roadside parking)	SP 115 066	163	SP 00/10
Cripplegate P	SO 831 086	162	SO 80/90
Badbury Hill P	SU 262 946	163	SU 29/39
Bath city centre P	ST 749 647	172	ST 66/76
Henley-on-Thames P	SU 726 835	175	SU 68/78
Cookham Moor P	SU 892 853	175	SU 88/98
Minchinhampton village, Friday Street P	SO 873 008	162	SO 80/90
Bredon village P	SO 928 369	150	SO 83/93
White Horse Hill lower P	SU 293 866	174	SU 28/38
Hughenden Parish Church P	SU 865 955	165/175	SU 89/99
Hailes Abbey P	SP 051 300	150/163	SP 03/13

Introduction

Much of the land covered by the walks in this book belongs to The National Trust for Places of Historic Interest or Natural Beauty. The NT has twin aims: to provide access to its land and buildings where possible, but at the same time to conserve the landscape, its wildlife and its architecture. This means striking a balance between utilization and preservation. Walkers can play their part by following the country code, and of course by supporting the NT.

The rambles have been devised with novice walkers and family outings in mind. But being a novice does not imply being careless or thoughtless. You need to plan your day in advance. First read the walk account and become familiar with the route on good maps. Next, check ahead on opening times and work out a rough schedule of walking, visits, rest and refreshments. Equip yourself with the right kind of clothing and supplies. Out on the ramble, keep your wits about

△ *Ashbury village offers rural memorabilia and a welcome rest point on the walk from White Horse Hill, across the Berkshire Downs via Ashdown House*

▷ △ *One of the NT's aims is to preserve our architectural heritage for future generations. This scene is near Beacon Hill, on the walk from Dyrham Park near Bath*

you: field boundaries may have been moved, trees taken away or new roads constructed.

To give you some idea of what to expect, the walks have been graded. EASY walks take around two hours and are generally well signposted along made-up paths and tracks. MODERATE walks take up to four hours or so; the terrain is mostly firm but there may be an occasional steep climb or rough track. DIFFICULT walks need careful planning, take the best part of a day, and demand detailed maps, compass, refreshments and suitable clothing.

The walks in this volume trace the course of our premier river from its infant Cotswold tributaries across aristocratic Oxfordshire, and through the Chilterns via Reading to Maidenhead. The mellowness of Cotswold stone villages nestling in their rolling hills gives way to the bustle of the lower Thames waterway as it approaches London. Along the way are routes to captivate the historian, naturalist and archaeologist – or just those who wish to get away. So put one foot firmly in front of the other, and repeat as necessary!

▷ *Cattle graze their way contentedly across pasture near Rodborough, south of Stroud. Their safety depends in part on walkers following the country code*

7

Countryside Care

The countryside lives and breathes. It is home for many, provides a living for some, and plays a vital role in our economy. It is also the basis of our natural heritage.

Those who walk in the countryside tread a tightrope: between access and conservation, involvement and interference, utilization and preservation. The NT and other organizations are dedicated to preserve our heritage, by ensuring access to certain areas while at the same time planning for the future. Walkers enjoy the highlights of the countryside at their leisure, but they owe it to themselves and others to conserve these pleasures for the generations to come. We have rights, but we also have responsibilities.

RIGHTS OF WAY AND ACCESS

Public footpaths, tracks and bridleways are 'public property' in the same sense as a road or car park. They are not owned by the public; however the landowner, while retaining rights of ownership, 'dedicates' a path or road to public use so that a right of way is established.

A right of way means the public is permitted to cross land by the designated route, without straying from it or causing undue damage. If you leave the path you may be trespassing; if you leave litter, or damage fences or crops, you lay yourself open to legal action. A right of way remains as such until it is revoked ('extinguished') in law, by the local authority. It is irrelevant how often the route is used, or whether it is overgrown, or blocked by a locked gate or a heap of manure. In some cases, however, rights of way may be diverted to permit buildings, roadworks or farming.

Footpaths and other public rights of way are indicated on the Ordnance Survey 1:50,000 (Landranger) series. In addition, public access is customary in common land since fencing it to keep people out is both legally complex and impractical.

Subject to the requirements of farming, forestry, private tenants and the protection of nature, the public is usually given free access to the NT's coast and

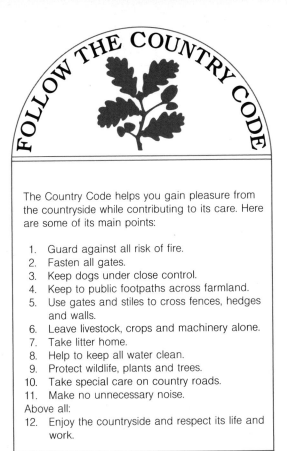

FOLLOW THE COUNTRY CODE

The Country Code helps you gain pleasure from the countryside while contributing to its care. Here are some of its main points:

1. Guard against all risk of fire.
2. Fasten all gates.
3. Keep dogs under close control.
4. Keep to public footpaths across farmland.
5. Use gates and stiles to cross fences, hedges and walls.
6. Leave livestock, crops and machinery alone.
7. Take litter home.
8. Help to keep all water clean.
9. Protect wildlife, plants and trees.
10. Take special care on country roads.
11. Make no unnecessary noise.

Above all:

12. Enjoy the countryside and respect its life and work.

country properties at all times. Of course the country code should be observed in these areas as well as elsewhere. Much of the NT's land is farmed, so take extra care to keep on paths in these areas. Details of NT-owned land are given in *Properties of the National Trust* and local publications.

BEWARE OF THE BULL
Complicated bye-laws cover release of bulls into fields crossed by a right of way. It is best to assume that any bull is potentially dangerous and to take a detour or avoid it if possible.

What to Wear

For all but the shortest routes the walker should be properly clothed. Purpose-designed boots and a waterproof top are not only sensible for comfort and safety, they also help you enjoy to the full your day out.

The first essential is some type of water- and windproof outer garment such as an anorak, cagoule or coat, preferably with a hood. Modern lightweight anoraks can be rolled and stowed away when not in use. For warmth the main requirement is several layers of insulating material such as woollen sweaters. These can be taken off as the weather improves, or added to if the wind strengthens. Wool 'breathes' to minimize sweating yet retains body heat effectively. A thick, warm shirt is also recommended.

Denim jeans are a bad choice for legwear. They are usually too restrictive and have poor insulating qualities. Walking trousers should be warm and comfortably loose to allow movement without chafing. On long walks carry waterproof overtrousers.

Feet are the walker's best friends, so care for them. Strong leather walking boots with studded or non-slip soles are the ideal choice. Good ankle support is a must in rocky and difficult terrain. For short walks on easy ground a pair of tough, comfortable shoes may be adequate. Wellingtons may be suited to very wet ground but quickly become uncomfortable and tend to rub up blisters. Whatever the footwear, thick woollen socks (two pairs, if possible) are the sensible choice beneath. Footwear *must be broken in* and fit comfortably before you take to the paths.

On longer walks it is wise to carry a few extras in your rucksack: a sweater, a spare pair of socks, a warm hat and a pair of woollen gloves.

▷ *The well-dressed walker pauses to consult the map.*
Many people new to rambling are surprised at how chilled they become after a couple of hours in the open air, away from warm rooms or the car heater. Even on sunny days the wind and a few hundred feet of altitude can make you feel uncomfortably cool. The moral: Be prepared!

⊲ The wisdom of being well prepared pays off when you get halfway round the walk and the rain closes in

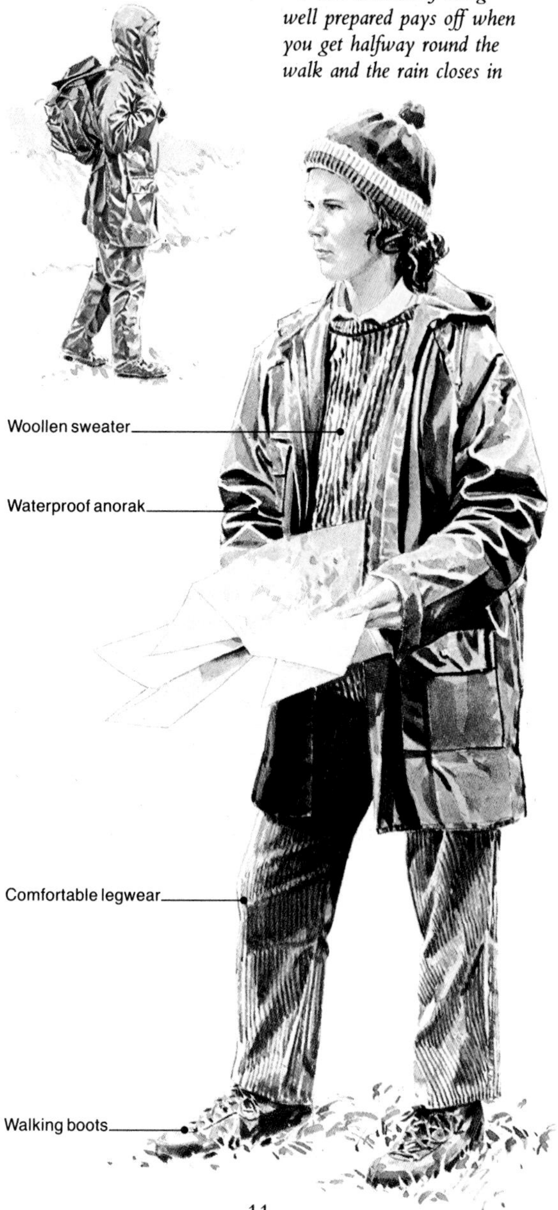

Woollen sweater

Waterproof anorak

Comfortable legwear

Walking boots

What to Take

Certain items are basic to any respectable walk. A rucksack and good maps are vital. Other equipment depends on the nature of the walk and personal interests.

The rucksack or backpack has many advantages over a hand-carried bag. With a rucksack you can take more, carry it more comfortably, and leave your hands free (an important safety consideration in rough terrain). There is an enormous variety of rucksacks available. For a half-day or day walk choose a medium-sized model of about 20 litres capacity, made of nylon or similar, that fits you snugly without chafing.

A selection of maps should always be at hand. Do not rely solely on the sketch maps in this book. These sketch maps are intended for use with Ordnance Survey maps (1:50,000 landranger series or, better, the Outdoor Leisure Maps and others at 1:25,000, about $2\frac{1}{2}$

▷ *A hot drink brings a welcome feeling of inner comfort on a long walk, while glucose or chocolate bars provide ready energy*
▽ *Don't forget the nature-lover's second pair of eyes*

inches to the mile). A good map provides details of rights of way, viewpoints, parking, conveniences and telephones, and lets you identify distant features (see page 14). A compass is necessary for map-reading since paths are often indistinct or routes unmarked across open country. Local guidebooks and field guides point out items of interest as you go, rather than after you return.

On a long walk carry nourishment with you unless you are sure of a 'refuelling' stop. Concentrated high-energy food such as chocolate or mintcake revives flagging limbs and spirits, and a modern lightweight vacuum-flask provides a welcome hot beverage. A few sticking plasters, a penknife and a length of string may come in handy so keep them in a side pocket in your rucksack.

Walking is an excellent way of reaching an unusual viewpoint or approaching wary wildlife. A camera records the scene and 'collects' nature without damaging it, and binoculars permit close-ups of animals about their business. Walk with these items at the ready – you never know when they might be needed.

A compass is essential; a 35mm camera outfit is less so, though a lightweight pocket version may come in useful

Maps

A walker without a map is like a car without a steering wheel. It is essential to obtain good maps, learn how to read and interpret them, and check your route before you set off. Most experienced walkers use a combination of maps, as described below. The sketch maps in this book are not intended to be your sole guide: use them in combination with Ordnance Survey (OS) and other maps in guide books and local publications.

The OS maps come in two main scales. First is the *Landranger* 1:50,000 series (about $1\frac{1}{4}$ inches to the mile). These maps cover the entire country and show footpaths, bridleways, rights of way, farm buildings and other features. They are useful for general planning and for gaining an overall impression of the area.

The second main OS scale is 1:25,000 (roughly $2\frac{1}{2}$ inches to the mile). These maps are published as individual sheets of the *First* and *Second Series* covering the entire country, and as large fold-out *Outdoor Leisure Maps* for recreational areas, holiday regions and national parks. The 1:25,000 maps are often called the 'walker's maps' since they show features important to walkers and ramblers, such as field boundaries,

▽ *In the National Grid referencing system the first three numbers are the* Easting *(left to right), the second three numbers are the* Northing *(bottom to top), and the reference is accurate to within 100 metres (110 yards)*

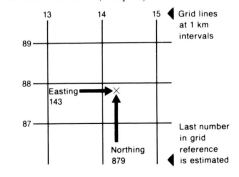

14

viewpoints, rescue posts and rights of way. Up-to-date 1:25,000 maps are recommended for use with the maps in this book. Further information is available from the Ordnance Survey (see address on page 127).

Another useful series is the *Footpath Maps* published by the Ramblers' Association (RA). These are at 1:25,000 scale and show many details such as footpaths, tracks, rides and bridleways, car parks and gates. For details of regions covered by these maps contact a local RA representative via a regional newspaper or community magazine, or enquire at the RA Head Office (for address see page 127).

Safety

Most of the routes described in this book can be completed safely by the average family, provided basic safety rules are observed. In more remote country, such as the Lake District, extra precautions are required.

1 Wear suitable clothing and footwear, as described in the next few pages.

2 Always assume the weather may suddenly turn nasty. Carry an extra sweater and an anorak, or cagoule, or even a small umbrella.

3 Obtain a good map and learn to read it. The maps in this book are intended for use in conjunction with detailed walkers' maps such as the Ordnance Survey 1:25,000 series.

4 On longer walks take some energy-giving food such as chocolate or glucose lozenges and a drink of some kind.

5 Allow plenty of time to complete your walk. A good average is two miles per hour, less if you enjoy views or watch nature at work.

6 If possible, have a first-aider in the group, and take change for emergency phone calls.

Chedworth

The historic Roman Villa at Chedworth, south-east of Cheltenham, is possibly the best-preserved of its kind in England. The excavations, reconstructions and museum offer a fascinating insight into life in Roman Britain over 1,700 years ago. This short walk, based at the villa, winds through Cotswold fields and woods via Chedworth village with its outstanding church.

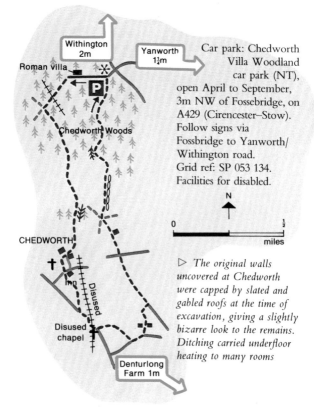

Withington
2m

Yanworth
1½m

Roman villa

Chedworth Woods

CHEDWORTH

Inn

Disused

Disused chapel

Denturlong Farm 1m

Car park: Chedworth Villa Woodland car park (NT), open April to September, 3m NW of Fossebridge, on A429 (Cirencester–Stow). Follow signs via Fossebridge to Yanworth/ Withington road. Grid ref: SP 053 134. Facilities for disabled.

N

0   ½
miles

▷ *The original walls uncovered at Chedworth were capped by slated and gabled roofs at the time of excavation, giving a slightly bizarre look to the remains. Ditching carried underfloor heating to many rooms*

The Roman Villa at Chedworth was discovered in 1864 when Lord Eldon's gamekeeper, digging for a lost ferret, came upon a mosaic pavement instead. Excavations began within a year and the site, now NT, is probably the finest, best-preserved and most fully excavated Roman villa in England. Starting at the villa, this 3¼m walk is through fields and woodland to Chedworth village, returning on a parallel route along bridleways with views of the village and surrounding countryside.

Allow time to explore the villa, either before or after your walk. Guide leaflets and books are available to tell its whole story. Suffice to say here that the building, representing a country mansion of its age, was in use AD 180–350 and probably occupied by Romanized Britons who lived the lives of country gentlemen. The total of 32 rooms was mostly given over to bathing suites, plus living and dining rooms. Much of the building had underfloor heating and there are exceptional mosaics throughout.

To begin the walk, go up the public footpath bearing left into a wood and going under a disused railway arch. Keep left where the path forks. After crossing a stile at the edge of the wood keep ahead (south) over two fields, then through a hunting gate. Cross a narrow field, go over the broken stone stile, and walk down a steep and slippery path south through a wood. Cross another stile into a long meadow and make for the village ahead. The stile to the right of a cottage leads on to the road.

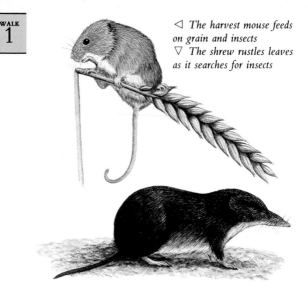

◁ *The harvest mouse feeds on grain and insects*
▽ *The shrew rustles leaves as it searches for insects*

Chedworth's Church of St Andrew is above this road on the right. Well worth a visit, the guide booklet sets out its history. The oldest parts are Norman, about 1100, while the tower shows evidence of being heightened several times. The three lower stages are original Norman; a century or so later a fourth stage was added; the fifteenth century saw its capping by a parapet and gargoyles.

Down a steep narrow lane on the left is the Seven Tuns inn, with good food and a delightful garden with a waterfall. Next to the pub are two stone gateposts. Go through these, then bear left away from the private drive to cross a stile into a long field. Keep ahead, cross the stile into rough ground, then turn right and walk up to the road. Turn left, and after 200y a former Methodist Chapel marked *Chedworth Silver Band* is on your right. Go through the small gate opposite and take a path at 45 degrees (east) down to the valley. Cross a double-stile in a low wall, then keep ahead over three more stiles.

Turn left down a narrow lane, bear left at the road junction and keep steeply up this lane until the tarmac ends between cottages. Continue ahead through a gate, then walk diagonally left up a steep field to a

△ *The disused railway arch at the start of the route*
▷ *Walk beyond the church for this view of St Andrew's in Chedworth*

double-stile. Over this, cross a narrow field to another stile opposite and turn left on the track. Note the excellent views of the village and valley on the left.

After ¼m cross over a minor road and follow the public bridleway opposite, signposted *Roman Villa*. Keep left of a wall by a small barn, then at the end of a field turn right to keep the wall of the field on your right. The path is invisible on the ground at this point, but becomes clearly defined as you reach the edge of Chedworth Woods ahead (north). (The woods are marked *Private Woods*, but the track is in fact a public bridleway.) Follow the track steeply down to come out, after slightly less than ½m, through the gate below the villa's car park.

An interesting addition to this walk is a visit to Denfurlong Farm, ¾m east of Chedworth between the village and the A429. At this farm is a self-conducted Farm Trail that describes dairy farming, milking (daily at 3.30 to 5.30 pm), crop rotation and the wildlife and conservation of the Chedworth valley. Taped commentaries, leaflets and an exhibition provide the information and there are seasonal data sheets detailing field usage. Further information is available from the County Planning Department, Shire Hall, Gloucester.

Chipping Campden

Of all Cotswold towns, Chipping Campden, south-east of Evesham, must be the finest and best-preserved from the affluent days of the local wool trade. This walk features a feast of Cotswold stone buildings and one of the most spectacular views on the Cotswold scarp, from the natural amphitheatre of Dover's Hill.

The NT has a large involvement in Chipping Campden, with three buildings owned and several covenanted. The 184a site of Dover's Hill is also NT-owned, and this 4m walk connects the two; the start can be either in the town or on the hill, with this account assuming the former. There is a woodland trail near the hill and occasional guided walks around the town during summer months. The area is full of history and provides an absorbing day out.

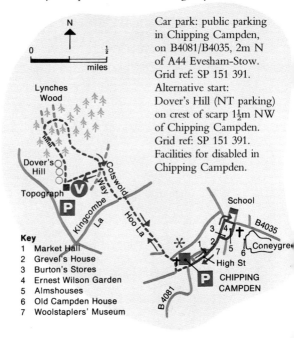

Car park: public parking in Chipping Campden, on B4081/B4035, 2m N of A44 Evesham-Stow. Grid ref: SP 151 391. Alternative start: Dover's Hill (NT parking) on crest of scarp 1½m NW of Chipping Campden. Grid ref: SP 151 391. Facilities for disabled in Chipping Campden.

Key
1 Market Hall
2 Grevel's House
3 Burton's Stores
4 Ernest Wilson Garden
5 Almshouses
6 Old Campden House
7 Woolstaplers' Museum

Chipping Campden's High Street must be one of the finest in all Christendom. The gentle curve allows the vista of honey-coloured oolitic limestone to unfold slowly before you. There is hardly a red brick in the place, though you do see some on the walk. People usually built in the cheapest material to hand, but the prosperity from wool allowed the more affluent burgesses of Campden to use stone. The quarry on Westington Hill provided much of the raw material, and now produces the artificial stone bricks of which so much of the town's outskirts are built.

Set in the middle of the High Street is the Market Hall with its open arches. It was built in 1627 and rescued from transportation to America in 1944, being bought by local trusts and transferred to the NT. It was not for wool, as sometimes thought, but for the sale of other products such as eggs, butter and cheese. The marketing of wool took place in Woolstaplers' Hall, now a museum.

From the Market Hall walk east towards the church, enjoying the different styles of building on the way. Grevel's House on the left (north) side dates from the later fourteenth century and was built by William Grevel, whose brass in the church proclaims him as the 'flower of the wool merchants of all England'. On the right you pass a road junction with the old water pump

△ *Chipping Campden's Market Hall, at the walk's start*

▷ *The Town Hall, with its wind vane and clock, marks the start of the Cotswold Way long-distance footpath — only 100m to Bath!*

◁ *St James's Church, Chipping Campden, soaks up the afternoon sunshine. Like many Cotswold towns Campden was a centre of the medieval wool trade and once enjoyed great prosperity. The NT either owns or manages several sites in the area, to preserve this historic and beautiful town*

at the corner. On the right-hand corner are the redbrick cottages mentioned earlier. On the left are stone dwellings which were previously a food shop – Burton's Stores. They were converted and a covenant over them given to the NT.

Several of the houses and shops in the High Street, including the Old King's Arms, The Plough and Red Lion Flats, have covenants to the NT on them. A covenant to preserve such buildings is a valuable 'property' of the NT in its work to maintain our links with tradition and the way our ancestors lived and worked.

Continue eastwards along the High Street and look for a wall on the right, with the church tower rising above it in the background. Walk through the arch and you are in the Ernest Wilson Garden, a recent creation from half of the vicarage garden. Ernest 'Chinese' Wilson was born in Campden but spent many years abroad, notably in the Far East; he returned with a large collection of plants new to this country, and this commemorative garden has specimens of the plants he discovered. Carry on along the High Street,

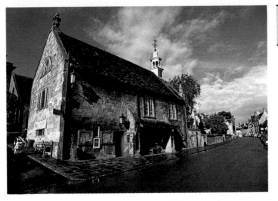

turn right into Cider Mill Lane, pass Chipping Campden School, and keep right to arrive at St James's Church. Beyond the churchyard lies the Coneygree, 13½a of meadow bought by public subscription and now NT-owned to preserve the view.

As well as fine architecture and outstanding brasses the church contains the elaborate tomb of Sir Baptist Hicks, who built the almshouses opposite. From the raised pavement outside them look over the wall across the road to the site of the Old Campden House, also built by Hicks but burned down in the Civil War to leave only two pavilions and the gatehouses. The pinkness of the stone still shows the effect of the fire. Below the wall is a place for washing carts, called the New Pool and recently restored by Cotswold Voluntary Wardens. The 'old pool' was in the High Street.

Turn right down Church Street and past the Eight Bells pub to regain the High Street. Turn left past the Woolstaplers' Museum; proceed along the street past the Market Hall and the Old King's Arms, now a restaurant and covenanted to the NT. Continue past the Town Hall (clock tower) on the right, which marks the start of the Cotswold Way. This long-distance footpath finishes (or starts) in Bath, 100 walking miles away! This walk follows it for the first 2m, and several other walks in the book coincide with sections of the way.

Walk along the High Street, passing Sheep Street on the left. By St Catharine's Church turn right into West

End Terrace. Walk ahead up Hoo Lane, which eventually becomes a bridleway up to Kingcombe Lane. Notice the use of the land; much of it is now changed from the wealth-producing sheep pastures of medieval days to orchards, vegetables and corn.

Turn left at Kingcombe Lane and then right to follow the public footpath signpost *Cotswold Way*. Continue by the hedge on the right to a stile and on to Dover's Hill. This site was the subject of another rescue by public-spirited people. A subscription was organized in 1926 to save it from hotel development, and it was presented to the NT in 1928–9.

Turn left to follow the edge of the scarp to the topograph, where the spectacular view is explained. The sweep of the Vale of Evesham in front is bounded on the left by the Malverns and on the right by Meon Hill, the most northerly of the Cotswold outliers.

This scarp and the area below were the site for Robert Dover's 'Cotswold Olympicks'. Started by Dover in 1612, they continued until 1852. At this time the railway was built through Campden, and the

◁ *Many buildings in Chipping Campden High Street display the mellow and mature Cotswold stone for which the area is famous. 'Cots' is derived from an old Saxon term for sheepfolds, while 'wolds' refers to open, undulating land; though the age of sheep has largely passed, the hills are now world-famous for their oolitic limestone*

▷ *Shrubs and wildflowers jostle each other on the bridlepath up to Kingcombe Lane* navvies and rowdier elements from the cities were able to attend. The disruption and debauchery were thought so great that the event was stopped – after 240 years! The Games were revived in 1951 for the Festival of Britain, and are now held annually on the Friday after Spring Bank Holiday Monday. Even without debauchery they are still great fun, with modern entertainments interspersed with old-fashioned shin-kicking! The torchlight procession after nightfall into Campden is unforgettable.

Below the scarp is Lynches Wood, and a woodland nature trail through it has been prepared by the NT. This part of the walk will take about an hour and may be muddy, so do not start on it unless you have time and suitable footwear.

To reach the nature trail, follow an easy route down the scarp as indicated by marker posts. The first oak post is a few feet south-west of the topograph. About 50y down the slope the second marker post turns you 90 degrees right, to continue under the scarp for nearly $\frac{1}{4}$m to the third post, situated beside a prominent oak tree. Try to keep just above the line of springs on this section. These springs are interesting geologically since they mark a narrow band of Cotteswold Sand. Water drains through the top stratum of oolitic limestone (inferior oolite) and collects in the sand because the stratum underneath is impervious lias clay.

At the third marker point veer half-left and you reach the flat lower pasture, in the extreme west corner of which the woodland trail starts at an NT sign.

The green woodpecker does not 'drum' as much as its relatives; it prefers a loud, raucous laugh

The larch and beech plantation on your left, a good habitat for small birds, consists of obviously man-made terraces. They are now very overgrown, but according to local legend were once a Roman vineyard. A Romano-British grave was uncovered higher up the scarp and experts suggest that the lower pasture might well be the site of a small Roman villa.

Continue along the nature trail (now marked by yellow signs) with the wire fence on your left. Along this stretch are buckthorn, food plant of brimstone butterfly caterpillars, and many wild roses. The nature trail turns left down a long flight of steps and the old trunks on your right are a favourite haunt of green woodpeckers. At the bottom of the steps you turn right and shortly join an avenue of very old sweet chestnuts, the origin of which is not clear. Look for grey squirrels along this stretch. Dense growths of self-seeded laurel provide cover for many small mammals and birds.

The nature trail turns sharp right, leaving the old bridlepath, and shortly crosses another old track. Along this stretch look for many fungi on fallen trees, especially clumps of sulphur-tuft. Continue round in an arc into an older, established part of the wood, probably the most interesting part of the trail. You

△ Substantial three-bar-and-step stile on the section between Kingcombe Lane and Dover's Hill. This is a traditional design, built to blend with the surroundings. In much of the area, sheep of medieval days have been replaced by crops

△ Evening closes in on the open pasture adjoining the approach route to the Dover's Hill topograph. The site lies on a spur of the Cotswolds and forms an amphitheatre where Robert Dover started his 'Cotswold Olympicks' in 1612

may see badger diggings, squirrel dreys, bluebells, yellow archangel, moschatel, goldilocks buttercup, wood sedge and sanicle.

Emerging from the wood, you see a sunken 'lane' on your left; this is the old track from Weston to Campden via Bold Gap. Roe and muntjac deer have been seen around this area. At the stile, look for another marker post some 100y straight ahead. Follow the arrow direction up the slope to Bold Gap. Near the top, at the last marker post, turn half-right up the steep little path back on to the edge of the scarp. At the end of the trees on your left is the stile where you emerged on to Dover's Hill.

The return leg to Chipping Campden retraces the outward section along the Cotswold Way.

Dyrham Park

From the magnificent house and gardens in
Dyrham Park, north of Bath, this walk winds
north-east through valley and plateau
countryside and the Beacon Lane plantation to
the attractive village of West Littleton. There
are wide views across Wiltshire,
Gloucestershire and Avon, extending on a
clear day to the Welsh mountains.

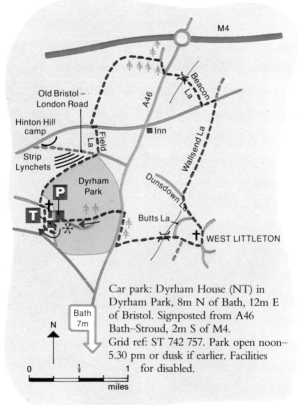

M4

Old Bristol –
London Road

A46

Beacon La

Hinton Hill
camp

Field La

Inn

Wallsend La

Strip
Lynchets

Dyrham
Park

Dunsdown La

P

T

Butts La

WEST LITTLETON

Bath
7m

N

0   ½   1
miles

Car park: Dyrham House (NT) in
Dyrham Park, 8m N of Bath, 12m E
of Bristol. Signposted from A46
Bath–Stroud, 2m S of M4.
Grid ref: ST 742 757. Park open noon–
5.30 pm or dusk if earlier. Facilities
for disabled.

▷ *The great house at Dyrham*

28

Dyrham Park, famous for its fallow deer – one of the oldest herds in the country – is the start of this 5½m ramble through the country at the southern end of the Cotswolds. As you plan your day, remember to allow for the park's closing time since the walk takes at least three hours. Although the route is mostly on gentle country paths and lanes there is the busy and fast A46 to be crossed so keep close control of children and dogs.

The walk starts at Dyrham and there are several guide books available to tell you about the house, built around 1700 by William Blathwayt, Secretary of State and Secretary at War, and the deer that graze the 263a park. The house and its contents are full of interest and a visit is highly recommended.

Leave the car park by the left-hand exit as you look at the house, and walk past the south-east corner and orangery to proceed south-westwards along the roadway to the crossroads. Turn right towards Dyrham Village, and at the grass triangle turn right again with the sign *Dyrham Church* into the lane. Continue past the right turn that leads to the church, and come to a signpost to *Hinton Hill*, *West Littleton*, *Tormarton*.

Turn right along a bridleway – part of the Cotswold Way long-distance path, waymarked with its characteristic coloured arrows with white spots – and pass through two farm gates. Follow the path along the wall of Dyrham Park on your right. Cross the field and enter the next field through the double gates. Note the 'strip-lynchets' on the left; these are terraces cut into the hillside to make cultivation with the plough possible. Above these is the ancient Hinton Hill Camp.

◁ *Dyrham Church, near the start of the walk, and worth the short detour to visit it*

▷ *The fallow deer that graze in Dyrham Park belong to one of the oldest herds in the country. Fallow deer may have been native in prehistoric times, but the Romans probably brought with them the ancestors of our modern herds*

▷ ▽ *Cattle share the park with deer. The mature trees show the browse line where the latter nibble at leaves and shoots; saplings must be protected in wooden cages*

Walk on north-eastwards to a hunting gate, go through the next field with Dyrham's wall still on your right, and arrive at a road, Field Lane. The footpath you can see through the farm gate immediately on your left, which aims towards the line of trees on Hinton Hill to the west, marks the way of the old Bristol-London road.

Turn left into Field Lane, walk north to the T-junction, turn left and enter the footpath to your right after just a few yards. With a hedge on your left, continue north through two fields, under electricity lines. At the end of the second field turn sharp right and follow the hedge on the right up the hill towards woodland. This is Beacon Lane plantation; follow its northern edge along various curves to a Cotswold Way marker post. Now turn right through the plantation and you emerge into a lane at the rear of the Avon County Council Depot. Turn right and proceed to the main A46 road.

Cross the road with great care at the southern end of the lay-by and enter the greenery of Beacon Lane via the stile by the right-hand gate. Walk along the lane and at the end of the wall continue straight ahead, over a brook and into a field with a hedge on your right. Go through the gap in the hedge at the end of this field into

the next and continue along the hedge, under the electricity lines, to emerge on the road by a gateway to continue the walk.

Turn left (north-east) and walk for 170y, then turn right at the footpath signpost into a bridleway. Head along this track to a gateway adjacent to bushy trees ahead. Through this gateway walk on in the same direction along Wallsend Lane, to its end at the junction with Dunsdown Lane. Go left here and walk $\frac{1}{2}$m along the road to the village of West Littleton.

△ Neptune and his fishy
charges are the only
remnants of the once-famous
Dyrham water gardens
◁ Church of St James,
West Littleton, has a very
large bellcote topped by a
pyramidal canopy

Past the village green and bus stop is a telephone
box, where you turn right into a footpath opposite and
proceed alongside the wall, through a metal gate and
into St James Churchyard. The church has a massive
thirteenth-century bellcote with a pyramidal canopy
on the east gable of the chancel. In the porch over the
south door is a pinnacled and crocketed niche containing a headless image of the Virgin. The church was
rebuilt in 1885; the adjoining Church Farmhouse is
eighteenth-century with Venetian windows.

Walk on westwards through the churchyard and
exit over the stile ahead into a fenced compound. Go
straight on and leave the compound at the footstool in
the fence. Cross the field diagonally, aiming for the
wooden gate visible in front, slightly to the right. Pass
through this gate into a narrow field, and through a
wooden wicket gate straight ahead into the next field.
Hugging the right-hand hedge, walk to the corner
where Butt's Lane terminates.

Go through the gap in the stone wall, to the left of
the end of Butt's Lane, into a field. Walk across to the

Lycosa amentata

Pisaura mirabilis

*On virtually any walk wolf
spiders lurk in the
undergrowth, where they
run down and leap on their
small prey with great agility*

Lycosa lugubris

bend of a brook running south-west to north-east across the field, cross over the water and proceed to a stone stile at the bend in the hedge directly ahead. Go over the stile, cross the field in a 10 o'clock direction (slightly south of west) and walk over the mound to find a gate. (Beware the gate at 12 o'clock from the stile, at a kink in the boundary – the gate you need is to its left.) Through this, walk on westwards with the hedge on your right towards the trees ahead.

As the path approaches the trees it veers left and comes out on the A46 through a farm gate. Turn right here, keeping to the grass verge, and walk for 250y, then cross the busy road with care to enter Dyrham Park. Go along the main drive and where it bears left go straight on, across grass and through trees, to Neptune's statue. This is the only relic of the famous water gardens at Dyrham; fed by springs, water from the statue cascaded down 224 steps to more fountains and a canal aligned with the door of the orangery, to the left of the great house. Descend the escarpment, cross the field and you are back at the house.

Bibury & Coln Valley

An undulating walk based on the River Coln valley and surrounding open countryside near Cirencester, on the south-east fringe of the Cotswolds. This ramble is particularly interesting for the many ancient paths and trackways encountered on the route, and the landscape generally is steeped in history.

In the course of this 5½m walk you follow or cross a wide variety of historic tracks and roads. These include footpaths used by country people since time immemorial across higher land, for the carriage of flint tools, salt or produce; Roman roads used by legionnaires and their supplies; greenways along which sheep and cattle traders herded their animals from Wales to London; farm tracks for the transportation of grain to mills along the river; footpaths from the outlying homesteads to market, pub or church; and, finally, main roads for travellers by stagecoach to Oxford and beyond. The NT's Arlington Row (cottages) and Rack Isle (water meadows formerly used for wool-

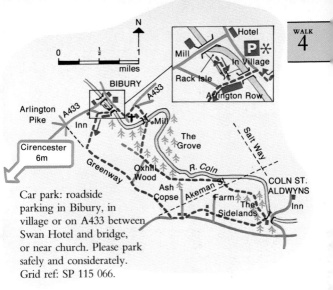

N

0   ½   1
miles

BIBURY

Hotel

P *

Mill

In Village

Rack Isle

Arlington Row

A433

Arlington Pike

A433

Inn

Mill

The Grove

Salt Way

Cirencester 6m

Greenway

Oxhill Wood

Ash Copse

Akeman St

R. Coln

COLN ST. ALDWYNS

Farm

The Sidelands

Inn

Car park: roadside parking in Bibury, in village or on A433 between Swan Hotel and bridge, or near church. Please park safely and considerately. Grid ref: SP 115 066.

drying) are near the start of the walk. There are numerous excellent guide books available dealing with the villages of Bibury and Coln St Aldwyn.

The walk starts in Bibury, at the ancient clapper bridge across the River Coln which gives access to Arlington Row from the main A433 road. Presum-

◁ ◁ *The ancient and ivy-hung clapper bridge over the River Coln to Arlington Row marks the walk's start*
◁ *Arlington Row was acquired by the NT in 1949 with the help of the Bristol & Gloucestershire Archaeological Society and the Pilgrim Trust. The buildings have had a variety of uses, chiefly connected with the formerly thriving wool trade. The dwellings as we see them today are the result of an early seventeenth-century conversion*

ably this was the only river crossing in the village for the pack animals with their loads of wool, produce or salt during the winter floods in medieval times. After crossing the bridge the path runs between Rack Isle, the water meadows on the right, and Arlington Row on the left. Arlington Mill, Arlington Row and Rack Isle are reminders of Bibury as a former centre of the Cotswold wool trade. Wool was processed at the mill, at the western end of Rack Isle; it was then washed in the Row, spread out to dry on racks on Rack Isle, and stored in the Row.

Rack Isle (4a) is now a delightful bird sanctuary, the home of mallard, coot and swan, while the adjacent belt of trees is alive with woodland birds. The River Coln itself is well stocked with trout, which can usually be seen from the clapper bridge as they feed lazily among the waterweed.

The well-known Arlington Row of cottages was a wool store in the fourteenth century and was only converted to cottages in the seventeenth century. Arlington Mill has now been converted to a Cotswold Country Museum and is well worth visiting, as is the adjacent trout farm. To reach the mill follow the path to the right at the end of Arlington Row, across a footbridge on to Rack Isle. The mill is 200y farther on.

The main route, after leaving Arlington Row,

climbs through a cutting and bears left at the top through a number of modernized cottages. It emerges into farmland through an iron five-barred gate and shortly passes a five-armed signpost. To the right, at the bottom of the hill, lies the Catherine Wheel, where pub lunches are available in the timbered bar or orchard.

The walk continues straight on, southwards, along what must have been one of the main access paths to Bibury from the wolds above it. You follow the line of the hedge across a couple of fields until, after 800y you meet the ancient greenway running from the Andoversford area to Fairford. A little way to the right this track crosses the Bibury–Barnsley road at Arlington Pike, a name which recalls coaching days. You turn left, however, and follow the greenway across undulating country, which can be muddy in parts during the winter. After 1½m it meets another lane running from Ready Token to Quenington. Just before this you cross the line of Akeman Street which ran from Cirencester (Corinium) to the other great Roman garrison at Alchester, just south of Bicester.

Turn left and follow the lane eastwards for about 100y, past two cottages separated by a farm track on the left-hand side. Continue along the lane for a few yards and then pass through a five-barred gate on the

left. (This is not marked by a signpost.) The path bears
to the right, eastwards again, as it continues across a
meadow. You leave a group of farm buildings on the
right and a cottage on the left, go across the track
leading to Coneygar Farm, and pass through a gate
into a field.

The path goes across the middle of this field and the
next one, and again this can be muddy in winter. It
then follows a hedge on the right as far as a belt of beech
trees, where it bears left and runs down into the valley
through one more gate, to the lodge gates on the
Quenington-Coln St Aldwyn road. From here there is
an optional visit to Coln St Aldwyn village.

At the lodge gates the route almost doubles back,
heading to the left (north-west) across water meadows.
The Sidelands, a fine belt of beeches, covers the hillside
on the left. After 500y the path enters the wood
through a gate marked *Williamstrip Estate, Keep Dogs
on Lead*. Another 300y and you emerge to follow the
edge of the wood to its north-western end. At this
point Akeman Street once descended the hill and

crossed the Coln. On the far side of the river one of the many Salt Ways from Droitwich came down to cross the river at Coln St Aldwyn.

The path continues for 200y to the bank of the River Coln. Going through a gate, you follow the course of the river across the water meadows as far as Ash Copse, ½m farther on. Go through a gate and follow the edge of the copse for 100y, passing through yet another gate into the meadows as far as the stile at the corner of Oxhill Wood.

This section along the River Coln has great beauty. There are usually large numbers of sheep grazing on the lush grass among the willow trees, and the woods bordering the meadows on the slopes of the valley sweep in great curves of green or gold according to the season. The river cascades over a series of waterfalls constructed for the benefit of fish and wildfowl. There is scarcely a building in sight.

▽ *Sheep take their time in the meadow below Sidelands*
The bank of the River Coln along the return section ▽

△ *The purple emperor flits around sallow bushes where she lays eggs; this insect is now rather rare*

The stile at the corner of Oxhill Wood is the traditional slab of Cotswold stone, the hallmark of all genuine rights of way in the area. You climb the hill and pass through a gate into a field. The path follows the edge of the field, with woods dropping down into the valley on the right. Glimpses of the river can be obtained along here in summer but in winter, when the leaves have gone, the views are much finer. Passing through a five-barred gate you follow a farm track for a further 400y, when it bends to the right down a hill into the valley once more. Views of a magnificent sweep of the river open up on the right.

After 600y you go through another gate and shortly afterwards wind your way through Bibury flour mill to a bridge over the river. A fine view of Bibury Court Hotel in its setting of trees, with the church and village behind, appears on the left. Follow the track straight on to the point where it meets the Coln St Aldwyn-Bibury road. Here you turn left and walk ¼m back to the starting point.

△ △ *The Coln on the approach to Ash Copse*
△ *A typical drystone wall and small barn*

41

Haresfield Beacon

This superb walk through woods, farmland and open countryside south of Gloucester provides a succession of views, including the River Severn, Welsh mountains, Forest of Dean, Malverns, Vale of Gloucester and the City of Gloucester itself. Three versions of the walk are described, each one crossing Haresfield Beacon and taking in a section of the Cotswold Way.

The NT sites of Haresfield Beacon, Standish Wood and Haresfield Hill (462a), between Stroud and Gloucester on the north edge of the Cotswolds, are the setting for this ramble. Try to pick a fine, clear day that will show off the superb views to their best advantage. The main walk is 6m, with two shorter alternatives of 4¼m and 3¾m. Most of the route is waymarked and part of it follows the Cotswold Way long-distance footpath. The initial section of the main ramble is by firm paths through Standish Wood, then by field and lane to the promontory of Haresfield Beacon (713f); the route continues along wood edge and across farmland in Harescombe Vale, and passes through Stockend Wood (also NT, 57½a) before coming full circle.

For the short 3¾m walk leave the Cripplegate car park by the V-stile on to grassland; turn right and walk towards the woods, keeping the stone wall on your right. At the entrance to the trees pick up the waymarks with yellow arrows and white spots, the Cotswold Way marks, and follow them westwards to the Trig Point on Haresfield Beacon. From here the route continues as described below.

From the Cripplegate car park entrance turn immediately right and enter Standish Woods, which are mainly beech and beautiful at all seasons. Take the left-hand path, which is the Cotswold Way. Follow it, watching carefully for waymarks with a white spot, especially at path junctions. After 1m, just beyond a farm gate and stile, the path veers right then left and on

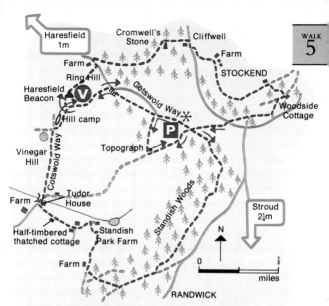

Car park: Cripplegate (NT), 3m NW of Stroud.
Take A4173 (Gloucester-Stroud) to Edge, turn SW
at fork signed *Whiteshill*, in 1m turn right signed
Haresfield Beacon, car park ½m on left.
Grid ref: SO 831 086.

△ *The sun sets slowly in the west from the Beacon*

43

◁ *One of the waymarks on the Beacon, showing the white spot and yellow arrow which is the combination for the Cotswold Way long-distance footpath*

▽ *Cotswold pasture and treed hedges, with the inhabitants enjoying the evening sun: a view looking south from the Beacon, over 700f above sea level*

△ *More Cotswold Way markers on the stile just beyond the trig point on Haresfield Beacon*

to a bridleway marked with a blue arrow. Turn right (west) here; in $\frac{1}{4}$m there is a small clearing where side paths join the bridleway, and you take the track forking half-right (marked with a yellow arrow). The waymarks now disappear between this point and Haresfield Beacon.

Follow the descending path, ignoring left-hand forks, and cross a broad track. Continue in the same direction to end near a group of farm buildings. Turn right and follow an enclosed footpath behind the buildings and then alongside open fields. The surface is rough here but gradually improves. Go through the farm gate at the end of the path and follow a grassy track with a wire fence on the left, down to a farm gate which leads between farm buildings and on to a lane. There is a lovely Cotswold house – Standish Park – to be admired here. Turn left and follow the lane for $\frac{3}{4}$m;

note a thatched, half-timbered cottage on the left, unusual in this part of the country.

Where the lane bends to the left, just beyond Tudor House, go through bushes on the right and descend the steep bank to a stile, then cross a plank bridge over the stream. Turn left and climb the field, making for a stile on the skyline and crossing another stile en route. In the top field climb over the brow, then aim for the bottom left-hand corner; climb a fence then go ahead, crossing one more stile (with a small pond on the left) to a farm gate that leads on to a steep, rough common. A track comes in from the left; turn right to join this and then climb upwards, until you reach the OS Trig Point on Haresfield Beacon.

This is the place to rest, and the most arduous part of the walk is over. On this promontory was an ancient hill camp which may have led to its alternative name of Ring Hill. The defence camp may have been used at a later date by the Romans; from here are wonderful views, particularly across the Severn Vale to the Welsh mountains. South-west is Vinegar Hill, which may have been a vineyard producing a weak and sour wine. Buzzards are often seen above the beacon while the scrub and common are home for many small birds, including blackcaps and warblers, and the autumn berries attract redwings, fieldfares and thrushes.

The full 6m route can be shortened here to 4¼m, as follows. Leave the Trig Point and walk north-east along the right-hand (eastern) edge of the promontory, crossing a V-stile beside a wicket gate on to a footpath. Follow the path to the road, then descend steps as indicated by the Cotswold Way symbol. Keep on the way, tracing its yellow arrows with white spots through scrub and woodland to open grassland. You can return directly to the car park or detour via the waymarks to the topograph, ¼m south-west of the car park, for interpretation of the views.

Back on Haresfield Beacon, the 6m walkers leave the Trig Point and bear left (north) to a stile bearing the Cotswold Way sign. Follow the waymarks, going north-east along a grassy bank with a wire fence on the right, then down a track to a lane. Turn left into the lane, then immediately right on to another track. Follow this track to pass Cromwell's Stone. This is something of a misnomer, since there is no evidence

△ In the Cotswolds and other hilly areas of the west you may occasionally see buzzards wheeling overhead in their keen-eyed search for rabbits and other prey. This, probably the commonest of our large raptors (birds of prey), depends so much on rabbit that its numbers crashed following the myxomatosis epidemic of the 1950s. Its cry is a mew-like 'keeuw'; when gliding (as above) its wingtip primary feathers are pointed back, while when soaring the wings are held forward and the primaries are spread

▷ Looking south over the topograph near the car park at the start

that Oliver Cromwell was ever in the vicinity. The date on the stone, 5 September 1643, marks the day on which Royalists raised their siege on the City of Gloucester, which was unusual in an area supporting the Roundheads.

Farther on, at the lane junction, is Cliffwell. This is a brick shelter over a well, built in 1870. The inscription is interesting but its origins are entirely unknown:

'Whoe'er the Bucketful upwindeth, Let him bless
    God, who water findest,
Yet water here but small availeth, Go seek that well
    which never failest.'

Turn right at the lane, then immediately left to Tump Farm. The next section of the walk is waymarked with a local sign, a yellow arrow with a yellow dot. At the farm drive entrance, cross a stile on the right. Walk ahead and trace the left-hand field edge, with farm buildings on the left. Just beyond the last farm building there is a waymarked field gate: note carefully the direction of the arrow before crossing the next large field to a stile. Go straight across the next field to a gap by a hedge, then follow the right-hand boundary to another stile. Walk on to a farm gate, then on to a farm track leading to another farm gate by a cottage.

Here you leave the waymarked route and turn right up a bank, just beyond a garage. Cross the stile and

◁ *Rich grazing on the path between the car park and the topograph*

△ *Cromwell's Stone. The date on the stone supports a connection with the Civil War but there is no evidence Cromwell himself was ever in the vicinity*

△ *Cliffwell, just along from Cromwell's Stone: can you decipher the odd ode inscribed thereon?*

climb the small field alongside a hedge on the left; enter the trees and follow the path upwards through a little wood. On the open area at the top, turn right over a stile and continue ahead along a path between fence and hedge. When you reach a track with Woodside Cottage on the left, turn right for about 50y, then just before a blue arrow waymark bear left up a woodland path. At the top there is a broad track, where you turn right.

A tree with two arrows is soon reached. Take the right-hand direction and follow this track until it bears left to a road junction. At the junction, take the lane signposted *Haresfield Beacon*, and in a $\frac{1}{4}$m you are back at the car park. After a rest, a visit to the topograph (as described above) is well worthwhile. Distant viewpoints can be identified, and on clear days you can see Dunkery Beacon, 75m away on Exmoor.

Estate management

Imagine that a rich old uncle passes on and leaves you an estate – several hundred acres of clay-based land. Suddenly you are the focus for interest groups. Walkers, of course, hope parts of the estate will be kept open and rights of way maintained as before. Horse riders are pressing for more bridleways. Local parents want grassy, open areas safe for youngsters. Conservationists ask for some habitats to be left alone, since they support rare flowers, butterflies and birds. The timber merchant has his eye on the trees, anglers want to fish the lake . . .

You quickly come to understand the problems of estate management. The NT faces such difficulties, possibly more acute because the public expects unrestricted access. There are so many aspects to consider. In the absence of grazing stock, and since myxomatosis decimated rabbits in the 1950s, open land is being covered by scrub and large trees. On clay the initial invaders are tall, rank 'weeds' followed by scrubbier growths such as the rose family (hawthorn, blackthorn, dog rose), birch and willow; eventually oaks predominate. Mounds of soil under the scrub give a clue – they were once meadow ant colonies. Some of the larger trees resemble hedgerow specimens with

full, rounded crowns; all around the younger trees grow tall and straight, crowded together.

To maintain mosaics of habitat and please both public and wildlife, some clearance programme is needed and grazing may be re-introduced. Ornithologists say that old scrub suits nightingales while lesser whitethroats like younger thorns: can we have both? Aquatic enthusiasts point out that ponds should not be allowed to silt or clog because frogs, toads and newts already have too few places to breed. Kingfishers and herons need to fish somewhere, while at night bats swoop after insects over the water. Entomologists are keen on ponds too, for the dragonflies who leave their nymph-skins on the pondside burr-reeds.

But what about the largest, most common and potentially most dangerous creature – the human? It is necessary to study its behaviour patterns, transport and habits, then to devise a plan that minimises damage while maximizing enjoyment. Most humans do not wander far from their car, or from other members of the species, and they like paths and signs. This offers a scheme: localize in one corner of the estate a car park, refreshments, grassy open area and woodland walk, and throw in a viewpoint and lake if possible. The majority of visitors will then restrict themselves. Often referred to as the 'honeypot' method, this scheme leaves the rest of the estate to the wildlife and those people who understand the need to conserve it.

△ A 'honeypot' – car park at Dyrham
◁ The patchwork fields of an efficiently managed farm

Badbury & Coleshill

This walk covers an almost complete selection of NT properties in the Vale of the White Horse, north-east of Swindon. Within this 3,620a site are woods, farmland, Badbury Hill with its iron-age hill fort, the Great Barn at Coxwell, Coleshill Park and Coleshill village with its beautiful cottages and farmhouses of Cotswold stone.

The Coleshill Estate, together with the Buscot Estate which joins it to the north, comprise almost 7,500a of prime landscape donated to the NT in 1949 and 1956 under the will of Mr E E Cook. The land is now protected and preserved for the nation. The gentle scenery is a joy for lovers of typical 'English' countryside. Farms, woods and villages are dotted about the Vale of the White Horse, with the Cotswolds north-west across the Upper Thames Valley and the downs of Marlborough and Berkshire to the south (see walk 12). Some of the paths on this 6¼m walk are across fields which may be under arable cultivation. In

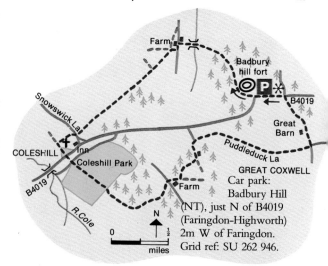

winter, therefore, the going on these sections may be rather heavy, and in summer walkers should be careful not to damage growing crops. Whatever the season, however, for the most part the line of the path is not difficult to follow.

From the Badbury Hill car park take the main path across Badbury Hill in a north-westerly direction. The hill fort is in the trees on your right, if you wish to explore it. Continuing on the main path, cross a stile to follow the grassy track through the woods; at first you walk on the level, then head downhill for $\frac{1}{2}$m. The last 50y or so of this track may be rather overgrown in summer. The path emerges from the wood into a field, follows the right-hand hedge to a bridge, and goes through a gate into the next field.

Again keeping to the right-hand hedge, go forward to a steel gate which opens on to the Brimstone Farm road. Turn left, and at the fork take the right-hand track. After a few yards go over the stile on the left and aim half-right across the field to a stile in the hedge. Over this, cross the corner of the next field to another stile. On the other side the path runs between a hedge on the right and a fence on the left to another stile. Cross into the next field and continue south-west down to a stile at the corner of a wood. The path then runs for 100y along the edge of the wood and the right-

△ *Approaching Brimstone Farm, a short way out*

53

hand hedges of two fields to meet Snowswick Lane. On this section there are fine views over Buscot Park and the Thames Valley to the north.

Cross Snowswick Lane and go over the stile opposite. Bear right across the field to a kissing gate at the end of a lane. In the field are the traces of a moat, said to have surrounded the ancient manor house. Below and to the west can be seen the winding River Cole, which here forms the boundary between Oxfordshire and Wiltshire. Turn left down the lane to reach Coleshill village and church.

Coleshill is an exceedingly attractive village of mellow Cotswold-stone houses. All Saints' Church contains architecture of many periods; although extensive alterations were carried out during the eighteenth century, a number of interesting Gothic features remain. The north aisle dates from around 1300, and

Cotoneaster is a hardy shrub suited to hedges; its sweet-smelling white blossom turns to scarlet berries beloved of many birds

◁ *All Saints' Church, Coleshill, displays a mix of architecture from many periods, from the fourteenth to the eighteenth centuries*

▷ *The base of an ancient cross sits on the green opposite All Saints' in Coleshill*

the south chapel from about 1500. There is a four-teenth-century porch and the tower is fifteenth-century.

On the green in front of the church is the base of an ancient cross. In earlier times the green was the scene of the annual St Faith's Fair. A few yards along the road to the left is an attractive inn sign announcing the Radnor Arms – a convenient midway point on the walk for rest and refreshment.

Until comparatively recently the main architectural attraction of the village was undoubtedly Coleshill House, a most elegant mansion designed by Inigo Jones and built in 1650. Sadly it was destroyed by fire in 1952, during the course of restoration work.

Cross the village green going south-east and take the road opposite. After 100y go through a white gate into Coleshill Park, carry straight on to a gateway, and turn right to pass through it. Follow the fence on the right to a stile. Keep in the same general south-easterly direction across the next field to another stile, over it and then bear left uphill to skirt the left-hand side of the clump of trees. Carry straight on to meet a farm track. To the south you can see White Horse Hill (walk 12).

Turn left along the farm track for about 400y and cross a road at Ashencopse Farm. Walk round to the left of the farm buildings and along the left-hand sides of two fields to a gate into a lane by a cottage. Turn left along the lane for 200y to a point where it turns right and then immediately left. Pass through a gate on the right and follow the obvious track across two fields to a lane – Puddleduck Lane – which runs eastwards for $\frac{3}{4}$m to the main street of Great Coxwell. Here turn left, and in 150y you come to the famous Great Barn.

The barn (NT-owned) is a property of considerable historic and architectural interest. It was built in the thirteenth century and formed part of a Cistercian monastery on the site. The massive oak roof timbers

are particularly impressive. The structure is 152f long, 44f wide and 48f high, and in keeping with NT policy is still used for agricultural purposes.

From the Great Barn continue northwards up the road to meet the B4019. Turn left and 300y of careful road walking will return you to Badbury Hill.

△ The Great Barn at Coxwell. Stone built with a stone-tiled roof, it was constructed in the thirteenth century as part of a Cistercian monastery and belonged to the monks of Beaulieu Abbey in Hampshire. In common with much of the Coleshill Estate it was acquired by the NT in 1956 under the will of Mr E E Cook. Its size is, to say the least, impressive — it is over 50y long

◁ The section from Brimstone Farm to Coleshill

Bath

This walk starts in the centre of Bath but quickly reaches the hilly countryside of Claverton Down to the east, to show glorious views of the city and nearby villages. The NT properties of Bushey Norwood and Rainbow Wood Farm are on the route, which passes through fields recently purchased by the NT's Bath Skyline Appeal.

This 6½m walk demonstrates just how quickly one can walk from the heart of a city to open countryside in many smaller English municipalities. The city in question is historic Bath, fashionable and aristocratic for much of its recent past. A note of caution: many footpaths described in the route are not signposted, so follow the direcuons carefully and make sure your maps are detailed and up-to-date.

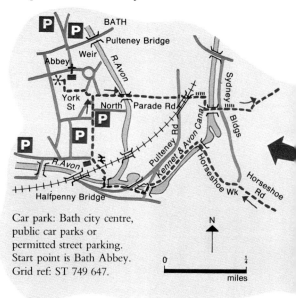

Car park: Bath city centre, public car parks or permitted street parking. Start point is Bath Abbey. Grid ref: ST 749 647.

A suitable place to obtain good maps is the NT shop in Bath, which is in Bath Abbey Churchyard and the starting point for the walk. The shop is in a large house, built in about 1720 and once occupied by Marshal Wade (a great builder of roads in Scotland).

Leave the Abbey Churchyard by the passage between the Pump Room and the Abbey, looking to the left at the decorated West Front of the Abbey. This depicts a dream of Bishop Oliver King, who was responsible for the rebuilding of the Abbey in 1499. To the right are 'Roman' statues – which are in fact Victorian – above the Great Bath of the Roman baths.

Turn left along York Street and on reaching the Friends' Meeting House (built in 1819) look at Ralph Allen's early eighteenth-century Town House through the iron gate to the right of the Meeting House. Continue along York Street and turn right into North Parade. Cross the road ahead by the traffic lights and continue along North Parade to reach the bridge over the River Avon. To the right, high up on the hillside, you can see Prior Park Mansion – now a school, but built in 1742 as Ralph Allen's Country House. Along the Avon to the left is Pulteney Bridge, designed by Robert Adam and built in 1770.

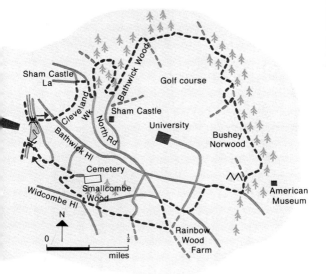

▷ *The NT shop at Bath Abbey marks the start of this walk. The building is occupied by the NT but owned by the Landmark Trust; it also marks one end of the Cotswold Way long-distance footpath*

▷ ▷ *Beautiful Bath Abbey, rebuilt in 1499 by Bishop Oliver King. Walkers may visit at the beginning or end of the walk – though boots are likelier to be clean beforehand*

Continue along North Parade to cross Pulteney Road by the traffic lights, turn left and then enter a passageway to the right under the railway bridge. Walk up this path, climbing the steps at the far end to reach the Kennet and Avon Canal. The 66m waterway links the River Avon at Bath with the River Kennet, a tributary of the Thames, at Reading. Turn right along the towpath and cross the canal by the first bridge. Continue ahead to cross a road (Sydney Buildings) and climb the steps to a path, to the left of a field. Carry on climbing, past allotments, to a field gate and stile on the right. At this point, turn left and leave the path to join the road, Bathwick Hill, some 20y away. Cross the road and enter Cleveland Walk, the road opposite.

Walk along the right-hand pavement of Cleveland Walk for about 400y, looking out for the Judas and tulip trees on the left-hand side of the road. Then turn right up the slipway immediately opposite Sham Castle Lane, go through the gate and, keeping to the right-hand edge, cross the field to a gate and pass through into North Road. Turn right (south) up the hill for about 150y and cross the road to steps leading to a stile. Climbing the stile, you are now in one of the fields purchased as a result of the NT's Skyline Appeal. This field is old semi-natural grassland full of wildflowers in summer.

60

Turn left (north) after the stile and follow the track, which stays near the road for about 100y and then fades away. As the track vanishes bear slightly right and make for a gap in the trees where there is a broken iron fence. Cross the railings and continue for a few yards to reach a sunken path going away to the left. Turn right at this point and walk through the trees to reach a large clearing. Go right again, climbing to approach a fence. Looking to the right a stile can be seen; make for this and cross to Bathwick Wood, also bought as a result of the Skyline Appeal. The wood is on the site of an old quarry, so there are few really old trees here. Most were planted or were self-sown over the last 150 to 200 years after quarrying ceased.

Walk into the woods for only 10y and then turn right. Just below is a sunken path broken by stones and tree roots. Follow this path, taking care to avoid the obstacles, to reach a stile. Climb this and take the next track to the left, arriving at the approach road to Sham Castle Golf Course. Turn left along this road and cross the golfers' car park, keeping to the left. Go to the right of the first gate, but follow the left-hand fence to cross a stile and join a made-up track.

Continue along this track until it curves right to a radio mast. Leave the track – that is, do not follow it to the right but instead keep straight on over the grass to woods on the immediate left. Pass through the gate at the end of the woods, then go half-right, climbing gently. Pause here to look at the view to the left. You can see across the Avon Valley, with from left to right the heights of Lansdown, Charmy Down, Solsbury Hill, Banner Down and Colerne. In the valley are the villages of Bathampton and Bathford.

Follow a faint track ahead through the grass, to meet a sunken path rising from the left. Now change direction slightly left, aiming for the left-hand post in a row of posts visible ahead. Soon you pick up a faint track and follow this through the gap in the trees. The path becomes more distinct, reaching a barbed-wire fence to the right. Follow it over a stile and 30y on take the path to the left, continuing to the top of the rise. Follow the main track, ignoring all paths to the left. This track goes past a rock pinnacle, behind which is a cave. Carry on downwards and then upwards to reach the golf course.

Walk along the perimeter of the course until you see a signpost ahead. Stay to the left of the open space to reach the footpath indicated by the signpost, and turn left along this path. At the next junction of paths go right and soon you pass through a gate on to the NT's 66a farm property of Bushey Norwood. To the right buildings of Bath University come into view.

Keep to the left-hand fence and follow the grass track to the far end of the field, then round to the right to a stone stile. Before leaving the field, look to the right at the various standing stones. The age and purpose of these stones are in some doubt: some authorities believe they are remnants of a prehistoric stone circle, while others suggest they are mere

▷ *A sight of summer: a bumble-bee visits the flower head of a woolly-headed thistle. The plant can grow up to 5f high and the large flowers are usually carried singly, one to a stem. It blooms from July to September and is found only locally on chalky soil. Bumble-bees belong to the genus* Bombus *of which there are about 20 species in Britain. They are often so engrossed in gathering pollen and nectar from flowers that you can approach quite closely and watch their mouthparts at work*
▽ *Views on the outward section where the route climbs from Bathwick Wood*

boundary stones. Cross the stone stile and pass a rifle range to the right. Keep ahead to a grass track just inside a stone wall alongside a road. Bath's American Museum is about 100y along this road to the left.

Turn right, keeping between the wall and the University playing fields. On reaching the signed bridleway, turn left and cross the road. Follow the narrow tarmac path to the University's entrance road. Cross this and keep along the path to the main road. Walk along the pavement to the right for 150y and at the road junction cross over and enter, by a stile, the NT's 296a of Rainbow Wood Farm. Follow the track through this field until you meet a wide track just before a gate. Go right for 10y to cross a stone stile into the adjoining field. Bear slightly right across the field and leave by a stile between a wire fence and a wide track. Follow this fence to cross another stile and then, with the new field fence on your right hand, arrive at a stone wall.

Turn right to cross another stile and then, 20y farther, turn left through a kissing gate. Follow the path downwards to Widcombe Hill (Macauley Buildings). Cross the road to a white-painted iron post with *Widcombe* and *Lyncombe* on it. This is a relic of the Bath Turnpike Trust, marking the boundary between parishes. Descend the hill to the end of Macauley Buildings, built in 1830, and climb the stile into the NT's field to the right. Now turn left into the next field (also NT) and keep ahead, gradually going right.

△ *The standing stones near Bath University campus*

△ *Recrossing the Canal near the walk's finish*
▷ *Bath, from Widcombe Hill*

Make for the stone trough at the far end of the field, and then turn sharp right into the field below.

Descend by the clear track to Bathwick Cemetery and leave by the stile. The wood behind the cemetery is Smallcombe Wood, also NT land. It is an ancient woodland site and the largest within the city boundary, with wild deer and badgers still in residence. From the stile by the cemetery, turn left along the road to reach Horseshoe Walk. Turn left, following the road to the bridge over the Kennet and Avon Canal. Go left along the towpath to reach the main road where you turn left along the pavement, cross the canal, and then turn left to descend the steps beside the canal lock.

Follow the canal as it passes under the road and continue along the path until it reaches a main road, Rossiter Road. Cross the Avon by the iron bridge that leads to Bath Spa Railway Station. This bridge is known as Halfpenny Bridge, reflecting the toll in days gone by. Follow the road (Manvers Street) directly in front of the station, back to North Parade. From here you retrace your steps back to the Abbey Churchyard and the NT shop.

Henley & Greys Court

The charming riverside town of Henley-on-Thames is included in this extremely agreeable ramble through some of the most beautiful Chiltern countryside. Beechwoods, rolling arable fields, views of the Thames Valley and the NT's Greys Court property combine to provide an excellent day out.

△ *The stone bridge spanning the River Thames, on the eastern side of Henley town*

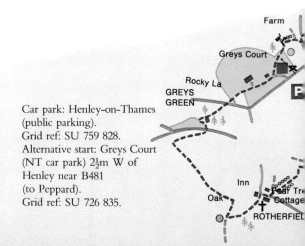

Car park: Henley-on-Thames (public parking).
Grid ref: SU 759 828.
Alternative start: Greys Court (NT car park) 2½m W of Henley near B481 (to Peppard).
Grid ref: SU 726 835.

This 7m walk may be started either at Henley or at Greys Court; the description that follows is based on the former. Henley is a pretty town with a good variety of fine old buildings, and world-famous for the Henley Royal Regatta in July. After climbing out of Henley, the route crosses the golf course at Badgemore, follows part of the ancient earthwork Grim's Ditch through Lambridge Woods and arrives at Greys Court. The return is through the scattered parish of Rotherfield Greys, descending through the arable fields and meadows of the beautiful Hernes Valley back to the Thames.

The walk as described here starts near Henley Town Hall, at the car park in Kings Road. Leave the car park by the north exit and cross over Kings Road into Mount View, following it through a right-hand bend to turn first left up a road with Mount View Court on your left. At the end of this road climb the concrete steps and turn right along Hop Gardens, then at the road junction turn left along Crisp Road. Immediately after house number 71, turn left and then right to climb through a field with a fence to the left. Look back for widening views over Henley and the Thames Valley.

At the top of the field pass through a metal swing gate and turn right along the road, continuing straight on at the entrance to Badgemore Country Club. When the road bends right (north) continue straight

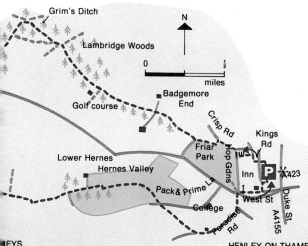

The swan's graceful appearance may tempt an approach, but beware: this bird is strong and easily roused

ahead along a track through Badgemore Park Golf Course with a strip of mature trees on your left, then after the last conifer bear slightly right to leave the golf course and enter Lambridge Woods ahead.

Keep straight on through the woodland, with the fence nearby on the left, for about 500y to a depression in the path. Join and follow north-west the ancient ridge-and-ditch earthwork, Grim's Ditch. Shortly, at the end of the fields on your left, bear slightly right to follow a waymarked path (painted white arrows) through the middle of the woods for nearly 250y, still following Grim's Ditch. At a prominent crossing of paths, turn left (also waymarked) to reach a road.

Make your way left along the road for about 20y to

just before the picturesque rose-covered Broadplat Croft Cottage, then turn right up a tarmac farm road for about 70y and go left over a stile situated between a metal gate and the gravel track to farm buildings. Follow the grass path with a fence on the left and a row of beech trees on your right, then after a stile on the left continue along the edge of the next field with a fence and woods to your right. After the footbridge bypassing a pond and another stile, continue along the edge of the next three fields with a fence on the right. ('Johnnies Gate' is carved on the gate next to the stile at the first field boundary!)

Reach a tarmac drive, and the NT's gaily-coloured ticket kiosk announces Greys Court. The much-altered house, parts of which date back to the fourteenth century, was donated to the NT in 1969 by Sir Felix Brunner. Inside are collections of pictures, furniture, porcelain, and the Carlisle Collection of miniature rooms. The house sits in a 286a estate containing various gardens, the Archbishop's Maze, and the Donkey Wheel and Well. Refreshments are available during opening times, there is a picnic site near the car park, and booklets from the NT shop give the full history of the house and gardens.

To continue the walk, go south-west along the drive and where it bends left, near the end of a gentle descent, keep straight on across grass to a stile. Here cross Rocky Lane and the stile opposite and continue south-west across the bottom of a small valley to another stile into woodland. Climb the woodland

◁ ◁ *Greys Court stands on the site originally occupied by the house of Robert de Grey in the thirteenth century. This was fortified by Lord de Grey in the following century, then rebuilt in the sixteenth century by the Knollys family*
◁ *The Great Tower to the rear of the main house is one of the few remaining sections of the fourteenth-century construction*

△ Early autumn in the shady woodland brings overnight populations of fungi such as these amantinas

◁ The stile at the cricket pitch on Greys Green, after a short woodland section
▷ △ Greys Green's green and cricket pavilion. Look carefully at the 'gate' on the right: it is in fact the stile shown in close-up in the photograph to the left

path, shortly to reach another stile into a small field. Follow the hedge on your left and emerge by a further stile at the cricket pitch in Greys Green, a delightful hamlet with attractive houses clustered around the open village green.

Now follow the gravel track along the edge of the green past Forge Cottage (once the blacksmith's) and at the road ahead turn right, walking along the roadside verge opposite. About 125y after the road junction ahead, turn left into a hedged and fenced bridleway. Follow this for ½m, and 150y after a right-hand bend, just before an oak tree on your right, turn left over a stile and go through the middle of the field. Head for a stile in the field boundary at the left-hand end of a group of trees next to the power line pole.

Continue through the middle of the next field, in the direction of the church, and after a stile and a short path alongside the churchyard wall, you emerge on to the road at Rotherfield Greys. The Maltsters Arms (Henley Brewery) is on your left and the attractive part-seventeenth-century flint-faced church of St Nicholas, in its well-kept churchyard, is on the right. Turn right and walk along the road for about 60y. Beyond the church are Pear Tree Cottages, built about 1500 and restored in 1947 by the Henley Housing Trust. The locked small building on the left, erected by Sir Francis and Lady Stapleton in commemoration of the Queen's Diamond Jubilee in 1897, has in the past served the village as both the well and a bus stop.

Just after this building, turn left through a wooden swing gate to follow the entire length of the path running between avenues of trees. Continue straight on, gently downhill, with a fence on your right. After the stile at the bottom of this descent, continue along the edge of the next field with a hedge on the left. After 110y turn left over another stile, then immediately right along the edge of this field with a fence and hedge to your right. After a stile about 60y ahead continue eastwards with the fence and hedge still on the right, then after another stile in the corner of a field, keep straight on along a farm track in the valley bottom.

▷ *Back into agricultural land again and heading east, after leaving the scattered parish of Rotherfield Greys and the tree-lined avenue leading off the road (below)*

▽ *Impressive trees line the route as it leaves Rotherfield Greys, with Pear Tree Cottages behind and the final section down to the Hernes Valley ahead*

Pass over two stiles below the attractive brick and timber house, Lower Hernes, on the left. Approaching the end of the Hernes Valley, pass over two stiles astride Pack and Prime Lane. This was used regularly in the days when goods were brought up the River Thames by barge, packhorses being loaded in Henley and taken by this route to Goring to avoid the long loop of the river.

Keep straight on between fences with the playing fields of King James's College on the left, and after a metal swing gate continue past cottages on the left and along a gravel track with allotments to your right. At the road junction ahead, turn left along Paradise Road and at the main road, opposite the entrance to Friar Park, cross with care and turn right. Soon you fork left into West Street and at the crossroads just after the Row Barge, turn left to return to the car park.

Cookham

The setting for this attractive walk is Cookham, the charming Thames-side village just north of Maidenhead. The route ascends the chalk ridge of Winter Hill, with its fine views of the Thames Valley stretching from Marlow to Bourne End, and passes through several of the many NT sites in the area.

Cookham, the Thames-side village of Stanley Spencer fame, is situated on a beautiful curve of the river to the east of Winter Hill. With the beech-covered slopes of Quarry Woods, the rural charm of scattered Cookham Dean and the remoteness of Cockmarsh, this 7m walk presents great variety and attractive landscapes. The route includes the NT properties of Cookham Moor, Harding's Green, Cookham Dean Common (including the village green and cricket ground), Tugwood Common, Winter Hill and Cockmarsh. The good and well-used network of paths in the area provides several opportunities to modify or shorten the walk.

From the car park, turn left along Cookham High Street for about 200y to the war memorial, opposite the Crown Inn. It is a picturesque street containing a wealth of fifteenth- to eighteenth-century buildings of

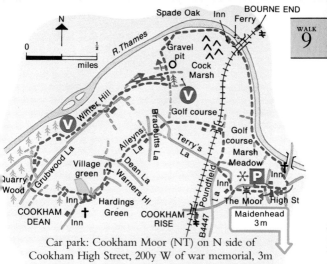

Car park: Cookham Moor (NT) on N side of
Cookham High Street, 200y W of war memorial, 3m
N of Maidenhead via A4094. Grid ref: SU 892 853.

▽ ◁ *The substantial brick
bridge over the Fleet*
◁ *Soft rush, common in
wet places throughout
Britain*
▽ *Spike-rush, also common
The water vole is often
called a water rat* ▽

historical and architectural interest. With your back to the war memorial, cross over the end of School Lane and walk back westwards along the south side of the street, on the raised causeway which has existed here since 1770. The brick bridge over the Fleet Ditch was a gift to the village in 1929, replacing many which were swept away in times of flood.

At the end of the moor (NT, 9a), where roads merge just before the White Hart, turn right into Terry's Lane. At the last house on the left, Tremayne, fork left into a short fenced path to a stile, and continue through the middle of a field to a telegraph pole in the far corner, at the junction of Poundfield Lane and Terry's Lane.

Turn left along the tarmac of Terry's Lane for 20y, then turn right along a gravel track to enter, over a stile, the John Lewis Golf Course – completed for employees of the Partnership in 1976. Soon on your right are views of the River Thames, Cookham village and bridge, and Cliveden Estate (NT) among the woodlands beyond. Follow the edge of the golf course northwards to the end of the fence on your left, then bear left across grass to reach a railway bridge. Turn left over the bridge and continue straight ahead through the middle of the golf course, passing just to the right of the building, eventually to follow a hedge on your left.

At a stile on the far side of the golf course, turn left to follow the fence on your right to a stile at a road – Terry's Lane again. Cross over the stile on to a path through the middle of the field. At the path junction in this field turn right and go over the stile, next to a gate opposite the white farm buildings of Hillgrove Farm, to reach Bradcutts Lane. Continue ahead down Alleyns Lane to a road junction at the bottom, where you turn right along Dean Lane for about 100y and then left, steeply up Warners Hill, either following the road or on a short parallel path across a small piece of NT common on your right.

At Uncle Tom's Cabin, keep straight on along the grass of Harding's Green. The road is on the right and you rejoin it at the end of the green. At the road junction after a right-hand bend, keep straight on through the middle of Cookham Dean village green and the recently-vacated cricket green ahead, on the direction of the Hare and Hounds inn sign. To visit the attractive nineteenth-century flint-faced church of St John the Baptist, or the Jolly Farmer for refreshment, continue on the road to the left past the war memorial.

When you reach the Hare and Hounds, turn right for about 15y and then go left into a path through a small copse. At the stile continue across the field ahead, with a wire fence on your right, to another stile in the hedge at the edge of a small but attractive valley.

△ *Church of St John the Baptist, Cookham Dean*
◁ *Uncle Tom's Cabin, approaching Cookham Dean and the NT's Harding's Green property*

Maintain the same westerly direction down through the middle of the next field to the valley bottom, and here bear slightly right up the edge of an orchard to a stile accessing Grubwood Lane. Cross the lane and turn right to enter and follow a woodland path (NT-permitted) between a bank on the left and Grubwood Lane to your right.

At the road junction ahead cross over to enter a narrow fenced path behind houses on the left. At the end turn left for about 15y, then right through a gap in the fence to follow a waymarked (painted white arrows) woodland path. When you reach a fence on the right, bear right between posts into a narrow fenced path. After passing between more posts you join an access track to the property Rivendell on the right; after 20y on this track, turn left to emerge on top of Winter Hill. This vantage point has, in post-war years, been somewhat marred by extensive gravel workings on the far bank of the River Thames.

Continue north-east along the top of Winter Hill with the road on your right, keeping to the grass where possible. Just after a dip in the road, 30y beyond the

property called Chimneys (formerly Winter Hill Farm), fork left down a broad gravel track. Shortly there is a stile next to a gate, over which you enter Cockmarsh (NT) – 132a of flat, marshy meadows and steep chalk slopes, declared a Site of Special Scientific Interest (SSSI) by the Nature Conservancy Council. Cockmarsh is part of Maidenhead and Cookham

△ *The woodland path on the west side of Grubwood Lane; this is a permitted part of the route, and approximately at the halfway mark*

◁ *Patterns with the plough, on the farmland flanking the route down into the valley and Grubwood Lane, after leaving Cookham Dean village*

Commons (total 848a) which, with the Lordship of the Manor, were acquired for £2,800 by public subscription and handed to the NT in 1934. On Cockmarsh are five ancient burial mounds, only one being easily discernible, which were excavated in 1874 to reveal the remains of two cremated bodies.

Just over 100y after entering Cockmarsh there is a choice of route. The main walk continues downhill, north-east on a chalky track with fine views over Spade Oak Reach. When you reach the bottom of this descent, turn left (north) over the stile next to a gate and walk through fields towards the River Thames.

◁ ◁ *Rainbows ripple the
Thames' surface in this view
downstream from the southern
tip of Cockmarsh, with
Cookham Church tower in
the distance*

◁ *After Holy Trinity
Church the walk winds back
through Cookham towards
the Stanley Spencer Gallery*

◁ ▽ *Church of the Holy
Trinity, Cookham, marks
the end of the riverside section
of the route*

An alternative route, for agile walkers, is the grass path
to the right (east) along the top of the ridge and then a
very steep descent between bushes to rejoin the main
route at the bottom of the hill, by a small gravel pit.

At the far side of the field, at the field boundary on
the left, turn right to follow the public path diagonally
through the middle of the field to the towpath. At
Ferry Cottage the ferry once crossed the Thames to the
Bucks bank at Spade Oak.

Keep to the water's edge and continue eastwards
along the headland of a field, through a gate on to the
north end of Cockmarsh. After another gate keep to
the path between the Thames and its riverside houses.
Among these is the Moorings Inn and Restaurant,
which provides a ferry service to the opposite bank
with access to Bourne End Station. After passing under
a railway line continue on the towpath for 1m until the
tower of Cookham Church comes into view immediately on the right. Here turn right to enter the
churchyard. The attractive flint-faced Holy Trinity
Church dates almost entirely from the twelfth century
and includes Stanley Spencer's *The Last Supper*.

To complete the walk, leave the churchyard by the
lynch gate and continue ahead to the road junction
opposite the Stanley Spencer Gallery. Bear right along
the High Street to return past the war memorial to the
car park at Cookham Moor.

Rodborough

This figure–eight route around the limestone-based commons south of Stroud offers a combination of walks, linked at the crossover near the Bear Inn. The going is firm and level while the countryside is high and open, making this a ramble for any season.

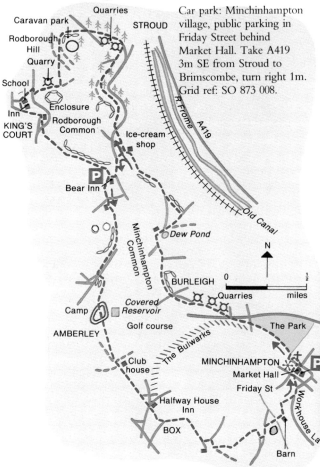

Car park: Minchinhampton village, public parking in Friday Street behind Market Hall. Take A419 3m SE from Stroud to Brimscombe, turn right 1m. Grid ref: SO 873 008.

From Rodborough Hill, 1m south of Stroud, several hundred acres of common land stretch southwards to the outskirts of Minchinhampton 3m away. This strip is 1m wide at Minchinhampton Common, but has a narrow 'waist' only 400y across near the Bear Inn. The common lies on top of a long, narrow ridge between the Stroud and Nailsworth valleys, with fine views from the edge of the scarp. The soil is thin and poor, on top of limestone, which is why it has never been enclosed and cultivated – although there are many old quarries. Today the area is of recreational value, and since the NT protects over 850a it will stay this way. The full 7½m walk goes round the edge of the commons, except for a diversion to the attractive village of Box. A short-cut at the Bear Inn enables the walk to be reduced to 5m. An even shorter ramble of 2½m may be followed by walking the northern loop only from the Bear Inn; parking is available near this hotel, on the common within 15y of the road. The going on all sections is easy, almost level and mainly over the open common, with hardly any obstructions. This is a good winter walk over firm, dry, short turf.

Leave the car park behind the Market Hall to explore the large village of Minchinhampton, built mostly in Cotswold stone. The pillared Market Hall is a notable feature and there are many fine stone houses around the market place. The church has an unusual spire, the top of which appears to be missing.

From the Market Hall, walk across the road towards the church and through the small gate into the churchyard. Follow the path up to the church and turn left past the attractive modern extension to reach the lychgate. Beyond this, turn right up the road and keep right until you reach open common after 150y. Turn left and follow a tarmac track along the edge of the common, known here as The Great Park.

When the tarmac ends continue over grass, keeping left. Arrive at a road, cross it and continue on the left-hand edge of the open land. The path runs along the top of a low ridge, known locally as The Bulwarks. This extends for over 1m along the southern edge of the common and is of prehistoric origin, presumably a defence line.

After 200y on top of The Bulwarks, turn right to cross the road just beyond a side road on the right. Go half-left and walk across the open common towards a pair of stone houses. Mounds on the right are old quarry workings, while on the left is one of the greens of the golf course. A visible path on the common leads you to the left of two houses. The structure on the hilltop to the left is a covered reservoir.

When you reach a lane by the houses, follow it in the same direction to join a road. Cross over this and continue ahead over the common. Follow a faint path about 20y from the wall on the right, passing a transformer post. When the wall turns right, you turn

△ *Unusual pedestrians take a stroll in Minchinhampton. The odd-looking church spire appears to have its tip missing*
◁ *Another view of the church, a few minutes' walk along the route*
▷ *There are plenty of stone walls on the route, many built with the spoil from the abundant local quarries; this one provides sturdy gateposts*

half-right downhill to aim for a stone house on a road. The views are northwards down the Stroud valley and eastwards up the 'Golden Valley' towards Chalford.

Turn left on the road, noting an old pond on the right in 300y. Water supply is a problem on these dry limestone areas and in the past farmers have lined hollows with clay to create such 'dew ponds'. Follow the road round a bend, past a stone house on the left and 100y beyond this, where the road curves left, you should continue straight ahead on the track. Keep to the left-hand of two tracks, towards a stone wall, with excellent views from this point. Behind the wall is an area enclosed from the common.

Turn left and follow the path until it reaches a road. Continue in the same direction along this with, over the wall on the left, an enclosed area recently developed as an estate of 'superior' houses. Keep left up the road, which leaves the open common for a short distance. In the Stroud valley to the right are the railway, main road, old canal, River Frome, factories and mills.

When the road regains the common, notice a useful ice-cream shop on the right! This marks the 2½m short-cut for walkers running out of steam, as follows. Turn left (west) at the shop, aim for a petrol station sign, walk 300y across the common to a road, and follow this left. In another 200y you reach the Bear Inn, a large hostelry, to pick up the return leg (below).

To continue the main 7½m walk, leave the road at the ice-cream shop and aim 45 degrees right across the

85

common, heading for a metal road sign. You reach the road by a metal water trough, cross over and swing right, keeping close to the road. A stone wall around a large estate appears on the left. The clear path passes through an area of trees, shrubs and brambles as it swings left along the wall to come out on the common.

Follow the contour to the right around the valley ahead. Join a clear path above a clump of trees, which takes you to the right on to a headland with good views over Stroud. Aim for a church spire and on meeting a path junction, keep right. This track leads down through extensive old quarries, now grassed over, to a road opposite a cattle grid. Turn left up this road, with woodland on the right and yet another old quarry on the left.

At the next road junction, go straight across and uphill to the right on a road towards the wooded hill. After 100y where the road veers left, take the path on the right and keep left towards the trees. This route leads to the summit of Rodborough Hill. Over the wall on the left, hidden from sight, is a caravan site. The track beside the wall leads to Rodborough Fort, a mock castle, built as a folly in the early nineteenth century. It commands excellent views over Stroud and westwards down the Frome valley to the Severn estuary and the Forest of Dean. Rodborough village lies below, with a pub, the Prince Albert.

△ *Conversation in the countryside: assessing livestock on the pasture land near Minchinhampton Common*
▷ *The commons near Amberley*

Continue to the left round the fort and join a track veering right, away from the wall of the caravan park. Aim for the left-hand edge of the wooded stone-walled enclosure, visible ½m ahead across the common. About 100y before the enclosure, turn right to a metal fence round an old quarry. Here the oolitic limestone of the Cotswolds, and the thin soil above it, are well exposed. From the quarry an old track leads steeply downhill to join a tarmac drive, which leads into a lane.

Turn right in the lane, immediately left over a cattle grid, and follow the road downhill. Keep left past an old school, just beyond which is the rear entrance of the King's Head Inn at King's Court. This unpretentious pub is a suitable lunch point after 3m of walking. From the inn garden there are views across the valley to Selsley Common and the village of Woodchester, famous for its Roman mosaic.

Go through the gate on to the lane below the inn car park and turn left. Follow the lane through the hamlet to the last cottage (Homeleigh) on the left. To the right of this building is a narrow pathway, which you take to reach a road where the open common stretches beyond. From the other side of the road the path climbs steeply out to the common. At a crossing track just before an isolated tree, pause to get your breath back, then turn right and follow the track over the common. While having your breather, admire the

view of the Woodchester valley below and Selsley Common on the hillside beyond.

The track swings left towards some large houses, behind a stone wall. On reaching the houses, it veers right along the wall to join the road just below the Bear Inn. Those on the short cut now pick up the trail.

Take the lane on the right of the hotel buildings and follow it for ¼m until you see Pathway Cottage on the left. Go through the kissing gate in front of this and up the path beside the building, then through the small gate and towards the top right-hand corner of the field. Negotiate a gap in the fence via a metal 'squeeze' stile, and turn left up a bank; due to a spring, this is the only part of the walk likely to be muddy. You soon come out on open common again.

Walk uphill, keeping right, and alongside a wall, crossing the drive to a large estate (Moor Court). Follow the wall until you see houses ahead of you. This is the village of Amberley. When the wall swings right, continue straight ahead. Turn left after 200y to cross the road and walk to the left of a stone-walled enclosure, and when it ends continue in the same direction until you see a large building, half-left and 400y away. Aim for this; it is actually the golf clubhouse. The mounds and ditches you cross on the way are part of an ancient camp, probably dating from the first century AD.

△ *Looking down on Woodchester, from near the Bear Inn*
△ ◁ *At the south-west edge of Rodborough Common*
▽ *The village of King's Court, displaying the mellow
stone quarried from the commons*

Pass to the right of the clubhouse and continue in the same south-easterly direction, looking out for golf-balls – especially moving ones! The large building that appears in front of you on the edge of the common is the Halfway House Inn, halfway between Nailsworth and Minchinhampton, on an old packhorse route important in the days when both towns were centres of the Cotswold woollen industry.

Go down the lane to the right of the inn and follow it for ½m through the attractive village of Box, full of stone cottages and well-kept gardens. Ignore all side turnings. At the far end of the village the lane turns 90 degrees left, with the drive to Box House (not a public right of way) straight ahead. Just beyond this bend, on the right, is a public footpath signpost, and you take the track it indicates. Just before a gate across the track, after 100y, go through a kissing gate on the left and continue.

Keep along the right-hand edge of the next two fields, passing through a small gate between them, to reach a lane by another kissing gate. Turn right, in

100y turn left, then left again after 50y. In another 20y you see a public footpath signpost on the right; cross the stile here and walk down the field, aiming for a metal barn across the valley. Minchinhampton Church is visible on the hilltop to your left, and a farm irrigation reservoir on the right. To the left of this, cross a fallen tree to a stile by a gate, go over a bridge and pass through another gate.

Walk up the next field, keeping left, to a gate left of a Dutch barn. Cross the adjacent stile and the right of way runs uphill, between fences, to another stile beside a gate. Having crossed this, turn half-left and climb a steep grassy bank. When you reach the top you see a gate ahead, in the corner of the field. Beside it there is a stile, which enables you to reach Workhouse Lane.

Turn left back into Minchinhampton village, and at a T-junction turn left again. Just before the post office (itself interesting architecturally) note an old stone house on the left, dated 1682 and with many old stone carvings. At the crossroads, turn right into the market place.

◁ *The commons near Amberley*
▽ *Common or viviparous lizard, often seen basking on walls in the hot sun*

Bredon

After visiting the NT's great medieval Barn in the village of Bredon, north-east of Tewkesbury, the walk goes over the top of Bredon Hill. From the highest point there are magnificent views over the Vale of Evesham and the Severn Valley to the Malverns, and on clear days to the Shropshire Hills and the Welsh mountains.

The NT's property on this 8½m walk is the great Tithe Barn in Bredon village, which nestles at the foot of Bredon Hill. The hill, an isolated outcrop north-west of the main Cotswolds range, gives magnificent views and supports a wide range of wildlife.

Leave the public car park, cross the main B4079 road and turn right towards the old village of Bredon. Arrive at the village stores, cross the road with care, and bear right into the old part of the village. To visit the thirteenth-century Tithe Barn continue to the church and walk along the path to the left of the lynch gate. Go down the lane at the end of the path and at the obelisk milestone, dated 1808, turn right. In 20y turn right again for the Tithe Barn. This impressive structure is 132f long and the stone chimney shaft serving the room over the eastern porch is unusual. Notice particularly the enormous pitch of the roof.

To start the walk up Bredon Hill, return through the churchyard and turn right at the village main street. You can see that both the first and second turnings on the left are along Back Street; take the second and keep straight ahead to a stile at the side of a gate. Go down the path to cross a stream and into a field.

The right of way now bears left across the field to the end of the hedge opposite, just out of sight over the brow of the hill. On reaching the corner follow the track along the orchard hedge, across the railway and out to the road. Opposite is a stile. From here cross the field, following a line of young sycamores, to a lane. Cross this and bear left to the entrance to a footpath. Walk along the hedged path and into a field.

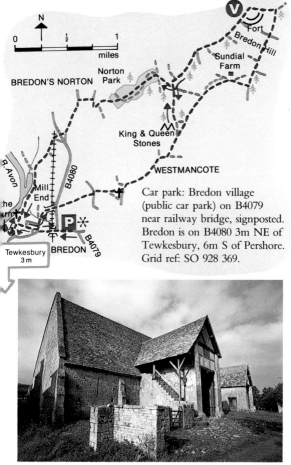

Car park: Bredon village (public car park) on B4079 near railway bridge, signposted. Bredon is on B4080 3m NE of Tewkesbury, 6m S of Pershore. Grid ref: SO 928 369.

△ *The thirteenth-century Tithe Barn, Bredon*

Ahead can be seen the end wall of a chapel and a wide gap in the hedge. Walk across to this and at the road beyond turn left, north-east through Westmancote. Carry on up the road, which eventually becomes a stone track, to a point where it divides. Take the right fork and continue to the right of a disused quarry, now a private nature reserve. Opposite the end of the quarry, at the old stone gatepost, bear right below a row of hawthorns to a gate.

Follow the track beyond to the remains of Sundial Farm. The sundial, without its gnomon (arm that casts the shadow), is on the barn wall. Go through the farmyard and continue eastwards along the track. At the T-junction, with the park wall and belt of trees in front, turn left. Now keep straight ahead with a wall on the right, for 1m over the top of Bredon Hill.

The name of this hill has an interesting derivation. 'Bre' was the Celtic word for hill (Welsh 'bryn') but the Saxons thought the hill was called 'Bre' so they added their word for hill, which is 'don'. Later the Old English 'hyll' was added, resulting in what we might translate as 'Hillhill Hill'. The views extend to the Black Mountains, 45m west, and Radnor Forest 50m

△ *The old stone gatepost just past the disused quarry*
▽ *Walking across Bredon Hill, after the camp remains*

Poppies lose their petals after only one or two days in bloom, to leave a seed capsule

and slightly to its north. Great Malvern lies 13m away, due west, and Worcester is 5m north-west.

When the path starts to go downhill, there is a wall across in front of you. Turn left to the iron-age camp. This dwelling was begun in the second century BC and enlarged in the next century. Early in the first century AD occupation came to a sudden and violent end; the mutilated bodies of over 50 defenders were found during excavations in a ditch near the entrance, which is over to the left.

To continue on the walk go round the hillside, with the wall on the right, to a gate on to a track. Follow the track and when the fields on the left give way to a wood, bear right to a corner where there is a bridlegate. Beyond here turn left and follow the wall on the left for nearly ½m until the path turns left down to the entrance to a disused quarry.

Those interested in geology may like to take a short walk along the path ahead to the King and Queen .Stones, situated just below the path in the clump of trees. The Court Leet used to meet here until about a hundred years ago, and on these occasions the stones were carefully whitewashed. To geologists, however, they are 'gulls', formed as follows. As the steep limestone hillside slowly slips and dissolves away, cracks are made in the hard surface rock. These cracks fill with small stones and limewater, forming 'nature's concrete'. As the hillside continues to erode, the pillars are left standing. After the detour, return to the quarry entrance.

The walk now follows the track down the hill, where long grasses and scrub are well suited to birds and butterflies. Go down through the park past Norton House (nineteenth-century) on the right to a gate. From here bear right, past the corner of the overgrown walled garden and veal and hen sheds, to a small metal gate next to a garden wall. Follow the drive ahead past the Manor House and old barn to the road in Bredon's Norton, where you turn left.

The narrow entrance to the church is on the right and at the T-junction is the village hall with its pleasant garden. Turn left here and follow the lane for $\frac{1}{2}$m to the main B4080 road. Walk along the grass verge to the right for a few yards, cross the road with care and head down the rough track opposite, which goes under the railway. In the field beyond, turn left to the second gate down in the hedge ahead. From this gate cross the field in front, keeping at the same height, to a stile a little way up from the bottom right-hand corner.

Continue along the bottom of the next field and then, after the next stile, keep ahead with the boundary on the left to a stile at the end of a road. Walk along this road, called Mill End – the mill, no longer with us, was at the bottom of the hill, and the waterway now filled with boats was the old mill race. On the right is the River Avon.

◁ *After the section of the walk past Bredon Hill's iron-age camp the route passes through agricultural land*
▷ *The oddly shaped King and Queen stones, visited by a short diversion on the return section. They are 'nature's concrete' left standing following erosion of the softer hillside. In earlier times they were whitewashed and used as a meeting place for the Court Leet*
▽ *The driveway of the Manor House, Bredon's Norton*

At the top of the short hill from the river is the seventeenth-century Old Mansion and Elizabethan Rectory with its magnificent stone entrance arch. This road leads round and becomes the main street through the village. Follow it and retrace the route back to the car park.

The Cotswold Way

The Cotswold Way long-distance footpath links 11 NT properties along its 100m between Bath and Chipping Campden. It starts beside Marshal Wade's House, which is the NT shop (though not NT-owned) in Bath Abbey churchyard, and ends within yards of the Market Hall (NT) at Chipping Campden. Both ends of the way feature in this book, in walks 7 and 2 and several walks cover sections of it.

From the Bath Abbey churchyard the Way winds through the streets of Bath, past the Royal Crescent and up to the Cotswolds western scarp. Changing views over the Severn Vale towards Wales greet the walker at many places along the Way. The route is steeped in history and full of interest for those who appreciate the march of mankind's development through the last 5,000 years. As well as living up to Gloucestershire's reputation – 'scratch Gloucestershire and find Rome' – there are 13 prehistoric hill forts to be seen from the Way. Of particular interest is the one at Crickley Hill, partly on the NT land called The Scrubbs. An annual 'dig' takes place here in late July and August, and visitors are welcome to come and view (details from Gloucestershire County Council or the NT's Severn Regional Office).

The NT has examples of later buildings on the Way at Dyrham Park (late seventeenth-century), Horton (the court has Norman remains), Hailes Abbey (medieval, dismantled by Henry VIII), as well as many open spaces with free access to the public at Westridge Woods, Frocester Hill, Standish Wood and Haresfield Beacon, The Scrubbs, and Dover's Hill.

The Way's route is marked throughout, apart from in the streets of Bath. It uses the Countryside Commission's system of coloured waymark arrows: yellow for footpaths, blue for bridleways. A white arrow is used on roads. This is a national system for marking rights of way, so to distinguish the Cotswold Way a white spot appears close to the arrow. Other paths and trails use arrows with a different coloured spot or a coloured tail, but if the white spot is there with the arrow you know you are on the Cotswold Way.

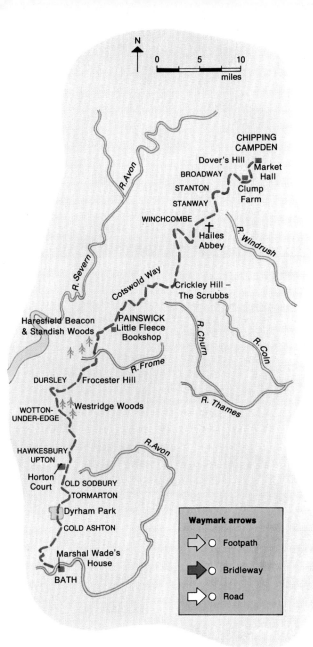

△ *Agricultural land flanks the Cotswold Way in this view from Dyrham Woods, on the section between Cold Ashton going north to the NT's Dyrham Park. Much of the sheep pasture that brought prosperity to the Cotswold wool merchants in medieval times has now been replaced by crops*

▷ *Sunset on the path to Marshfield, one of the many spurs of the Cotswold Way. This long-distance path is within easy reach of numerous villages and towns, where walkers exploring its entire length may find refreshment and overnight accommodation*

Maintenance and waymarking of the Way is a joint venture between the Cotswold Voluntary Warden Service and the Ramblers' Association. These volunteers surveyed the route and consulted the many landowners before placing waymarks, and they now continuously maintain the marks and the condition of the paths.

A general description of the Cotswold Way is contained in the NT's *Book of Long Walks*. Other guides to the Way are *The Cotswold Way – The Complete Walker's Guide* by Mark Richards and *A Guide to the Cotswold Way* by Richard Sale. As well as navigational detail, both are packed with information and pictures. Details of accommodation and transport are contained in *The Cotswold Way Handbook* produced by the Ramblers' Association in Gloucestershire and available via local RA representatives.

White Horse Hill

This long, high walk on the Berkshire Downs reveals panoramic views north over the Vale of the White Horse and south over Lambourn. Part of the route follows the Ridgeway Path.

Allow extra time for an exploration of the archaeological features on White Horse Hill, a visit to Ashdown House, and a recommended detour to Ashbury for refreshments.

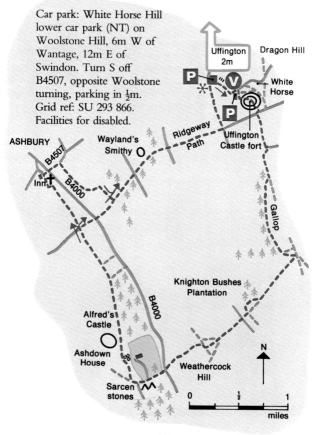

Car park: White Horse Hill lower car park (NT) on Woolstone Hill, 6m W of Wantage, 12m E of Swindon. Turn S off B4507, opposite Woolstone turning, parking in ½m. Grid ref: SU 293 866. Facilities for disabled.

Uffington 2m

Dragon Hill

White Horse

Ridgeway Path

Uffington Castle fort

ASHBURY

B4507

Wayland's Smithy

Inn

B4000

Gallop

Knighton Bushes Plantation

B4000

Alfred's Castle

Ashdown House

Weathercock Hill

Sarcen stones

N

0   ½   1
miles

Most of this 9m walk is above the 500f contour level. Large sections of the route are open to the elements and there are fine views over the Vale of the White Horse and the Lambourn Downs, so try to choose a clear, dry day. Generally the route is easy to follow; allow an extra two or three hours, on top of the walking time of $4\frac{1}{2}$ hours, for detours and explorations.

Leave the lower White Horse Hill car park by the steps on the far side. Head up the hill in a south-easterly direction to the viewpoint indicator, a gift of the Royal Military College of Science. Go through the gate a few yards to the south and turn left along Dragonhill Road to the upper car park, which is reserved for the elderly and disabled. Take any of the paths leading up to the 'castle' and the White Horse is just below, cut into the chalk of the north-east slope.

There are three features on the 856f White Horse Hill: the White Horse itself, Uffington Castle and Dragon Hill. The 235a are owned by the NT but are in the care of the Historic Buildings and Monuments Commission.

The White Horse is 360f long. Its origin is uncertain; it may date from Saxon times, but there are indications that it was constructed during the iron age. Uffington Castle is an ancient hill fort, roughly circular and about 250y in diameter. It is also of uncertain origin but the

△ *Uffington 'Castle' (hill fort) on White Horse Hill*

site was occupied at least as far back as 300 BC. Below, ½m to the north-east, lies the natural flat-topped hillock of Dragon Hill – the legendary location of St George's slaying of the dragon.

Leave the castle by the gap in the bank on the south side. Go over a stile a few yards to the left to join the Ridgeway Path long-distance footpath. Turn right (west) and after 20y turn left along the signposted bridleway. This follows the right-hand boundary of a large field for about ½m and then goes left at the corner for 40y to a gate. Go through and keep on southwards, down a well-defined track for 400y to a belt of trees on the right. Bear right just beyond the trees. The path curves round to continue in a southerly direction across Woolstone Down, alongside a gallop on the left.

After ¾m the route swings half-left for 250y to a junction of several paths. Here turn sharp right, taking the track running downhill in a south-westerly direction. After ½m the track curves to the right to skirt Knighton Bushes Plantation but then continues in the same south-westerly direction for another ½m to a T-junction at the top of a hill. Strike half-right across a field, making for the left-hand of two trees. This is Weathercock Hill. Spare a moment to glance back at the view of White Horse Hill and then look ahead to Ashdown House.

△ *The grass snake, our largest snake species*

△ ◁ *View west from the path on Uffington Down, to Woolstone Hill Barn*

△ *Ashdown House (NT) has been described as 'the perfect doll's house'*

At the far side of the field go through the wicket gate to the next field. Walk downhill by the left-hand fence to a fixed gate, climb this and the steel gate next to it, and enter the field on the left. Continue downhill to a stile by the B4000 road. Cross over and follow the lane opposite, which in 300y arrives at the entrance to Ashdown House. Note the sarsen stones, relics from the glacial period, in the fields on either side.

Ashdown House and the surrounding 40a of parkland are NT-owned. The building of the house was commissioned by the First Lord Craven in 1660 for Elizabeth of Bohemia, sister of Charles I, but she died before it was completed. The house has been described by Pevsner as 'the perfect doll's house'. It is constructed of chalk blocks with stone quoins (corner keystones), and rises to four storeys. Inside, a massive oak staircase occupies nearly a quarter of the floor area and is hung with portraits of the Craven family.

About 200y past the entrance to the house the lane turns sharp left, but you continue along the track ahead. In 50y where the track forks, go through the gate to the right and walk up the right-hand field boundary. Note the avenue of limes.

At the top of the field is Alfred's Castle. Despite its name, this earthwork is pre-Saxon. There is evidence that it was occupied by iron-age people, and then later by Romans and Saxons. From Alfred's Castle a steel gate leads into a long narrow field. Keep to the middle of this for 500y; the path then continues along the left-hand fence to another steel gate. Here the path becomes a well defined track which, after $\frac{3}{4}$m heading north-west, joins the Ridgeway. Turn right here for the main route.

A detour to obtain refreshment in Ashbury, which lengthens the walk by $1\frac{1}{2}$m, can be made at the point where you join the Ridgeway. Cross directly over to a path which continues north-west and drops down towards the village. Just before the church, where the

path forks, bear left through the churchyard to a lane leading to the village and the Rose and Crown inn. Suitably fed and watered, turn eastwards along the B4507 road, cross the B4000, and 200y farther on turn right on to the signposted footpath that takes you south-east, to regain the Ridgeway in ¾m.

Once on the Ridgeway continue north-east for 1m to reach Wayland's Smithy, a neolithic burial site dating from around 3,500 BC. The name derives from a smithy with magical powers, a story which Sir Walter Scott brought into the plot of *Kenilworth*. Continue along the Ridgeway for another 1m to a crossing track where the Ridgeway ahead begins to climb up to White Horse Hill. Turn left here for ½m to return to the lower car park.

▷ *Wayland's Smithy, an ancient burial site*
▽ ◁ *The pretty village of Ashbury and its inn offer refreshment and rest after two-thirds of the route*
▽ *From the Ridgeway near Ashbury natural hues contrast with monotone of crops*

Hughenden

This ramble through the Buckinghamshire Chilterns explores the beautiful valleys, high ridges and rolling beechwoods north-west of High Wycombe. The route takes in three large and interesting NT properties: Hughenden Manor and Gardens, West Wycombe House and Park, and Bradenham Manor and village.

This 9m walk starts near Hughenden Manor, once home of Benjamin Disraeli who lived there until his death on 19 April 1881. The route climbs up to Downley Common before crossing the Risborough Road valley to the village and park of West Wycombe. After following the ridge through Hearnton Wood you descend into the valley again to Bradenham village, where over 1,100a including manor, farmland and virtually all the village are owned and protected by the NT. Finally you climb up to and across Naphill Common. The going is generally good but some of the lower wooded land may be muddy after rain.

To commence the walk, enter the churchyard through the metal swing gate and walk up the tarmac path. On your right is the attractive flint-faced Hughenden Parish Church of St Michael and All Angels; almost completely rebuilt in 1875 on the site of a twelfth-century church, it houses Queen Victoria's memorial to Disraeli. This is unique, being the only memorial erected to a subject by a reigning monarch. Outside, at the east end of the North Chapel, is the Disraeli family tomb containing the remains of the Right Honourable Benjamin Disraeli, Earl of Beaconsfield, and Viscount Hughenden, KG.

At the top of the churchyard, pass on the left the Church House – a monastic house until the Reformation, then much later made into almshouses, and in 1927 largely restored to its former picturesque construction and appearance.

Leave the churchyard by the metal swing gate,

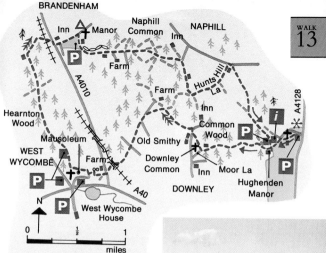

BRANDENHAM

Naphill
Common

NAPHILL

Inn Manor

Inn

P

Farm

Hunts Hill La

A4010

Farm

A4128

Hearnton
Wood

Mausoleum

Inn

Common
Wood

P

i

WEST
WYCOMBE

Old Smithy

P

Farm

Downley
Common

Inn

Moor La

Hughenden
Manor

P

P

DOWNLEY

A40

N

0   ½   1
miles

West Wycombe
House

Car park: Hughenden
Parish Church (public) on
approach road to manor,
just W of A4128 1¼m N
of High Wycombe.
Grid ref: SU 865 955.
Alternative start (NT
parking) at West
Wycombe and Bradenham

▷ *The Church of St
Michael and All Angels, in
the grounds of Hughenden
Manor. Benjamin Disraeli
is buried with his wife
Mary Anne in its
graveyard*

continue straight on uphill through the park to a
cattlegrid and gate at the road ahead. Here turn left
along the road to reach, at the top of a climb on the left,
the entrance to Hughenden Manor and Gardens. The
169a were bought in 1847 by Disraeli, who
refashioned the house and lived the rest of his life there.
The house contains much of his furniture, pictures,

△ *Hughenden Manor, bought by Disraeli in 1847*
▷ *Pasture near Flint Hall Farm, West Wycombe*

books and other relics, and there is an NT shop and Information Room in an old stable block opposite.

After visiting the manor, return to the entrance and continue between flint walls, walking south-west. Soon you reach the end of the road and enter a descending woodland path curving to the right. Ignore a path to your right and on emerging from the woodland continue on a fenced track in the bottom of the valley. Enter Common Wood ahead, still keeping to the valley bottom and ignoring all side paths. Soon after the isolated Well Cottage (1813) on the right, emerge from woodland on to the edge of Downley Common.

At the road, ahead, Moor Lane, turn right up a gravel track, passing nearby on your left the flint-faced 1824 Wesleyan chapel – Downley Methodist Church. Continue along the left-hand edge of the common to Emery's Dairy, then bear left through the middle of the common. You pass a cricket green on the right and reach, after a crossing road, a footpath to the right of The Old Smithy and the cricket pavilion. Go through two wooden swing gates to a small field, and continue ahead along the edge of a large field with a hedge on the right. Shortly, look left for the distant tower of St Lawrence Church at West Wycombe, capped with a gleaming golden ball overlooking the enormous Dashwood Mausoleum.

Entering Lee's Wood ahead, descend steeply to a path junction in the bottom of the valley. Here turn left

to follow the valley gently downhill. Emerge from the woodland by a gate, turn left along a tarmac farm road, then where the road bears left, keep straight on to enter the field ahead by a stile. Maintain the same direction through the middle of the field and, after stiles either side of the field track, continue along the edge of the next long field with a hedge and fence on your right. Near the end of this field look ahead across the valley for views among the trees of West Wycombe House. Home of the present Sir Francis Dashwood, it was rebuilt in the mid–eighteenth century in the Palladian style for the second baronet, and stands in a landscaped garden that includes an ornamental lake.

In the corner of the field bear right through a thick hedge down the edge of the field, with a fence on your right. After a stile and a gate at a railway tunnel, turn half-left through the middle of a field to a 'squeeze' stile at the A4010 road. With great care cross over to a stile opposite, next to Flint Hall Farm, and continue halfway along the edge of a field with a fence and row of large trees on the right. Pass over a stile on the right to put the field boundary on your left, and soon you reach the road ahead.

The main walk continues to the right, but it is recommended that you turn left to visit West Wycombe – a village of many historic cottages, purchased in 1929 by the Royal Society of Arts, and after repair and internal modernization transferred to

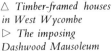
△ *Timber-framed houses in West Wycombe*
▷ *The imposing Dashwood Mausoleum*

the NT in 1934. West Wycombe House and Park are at the far (southern) end of the village on the other side of the A40, while at the near end are the Hell Fire Caves. These were hollowed out for road material in the 1750s by Sir Francis Dashwood (subsequently Lord le Despencer), and were used for the notorious activities of the Hell Fire Club.

To continue the walk, turn right along the road for about 20y, then fork left up a bank and through a 'stileway' to climb the grass path up to the impressive stone-and-flint Dashwood Mausoleum, built in 1763 to house memorials to the Despencer family. Beyond the mausoleum is the West Wycombe Parish Church of St Lawrence, largely rebuilt in the mid-eighteenth century from the original thirteenth-century Norman. Its nave is quite startling with its ornate plasterwork and painted ceiling. A small fee towards church maintenance allows you to ascend the tower.

Leave the churchyard by its gravel drive and wooden gate in the far corner, and continue along the ridge through a car park to take a track into Hearnton

Early-morning or late-evening walkers will be familiar with the ubiquitous hedgehog

WALK
13

Wood, to the left of a red-and-white building ahead. Follow this track along the top of the ridge for about 1m, through a mixture of mature woodland, fields and newly-created plantations. Eventually you reach a brick-and-flint house on the left, recently reclaimed from the former derelict buildings of Nobles Farm. Immediately after this building, turn right steeply downhill along the edge of mature woodland with a fence on the right. After 100y bear left through the woodland, shortly to enter a field ahead by a stile. Pause here for a distant view through the trees of the village of Bradenham, one of the most unspoilt of Chiltern villages with its attractive seventeenth-century Manor House overlooking the large village green.

Continue downhill with a hedge on your right, and after passing through the middle of the second field, cross the railway with great care using the stiles on each side. After another small field and a metal swing gate, carefully cross over the main A4010 road again and turn right for about 50y. Go left at the Red Lion to enter Bradenham village. The NT protects almost all of the village, the Manor House, five farms and 380a of woods.

Shortly keep to the left side of the green and at the far end of the village you find the Old School House, now a Youth Hostel, and the flint-faced Parish Church of St Botolph. This claims to have two of the oldest bells in the country. Now turn right across the end of the green to pass in front of the Manor House – once the home of the writer Isaac Disraeli and his son Benjamin (who later became Prime Minister), and now let as a conference centre.

113

△ *Bradenham village is about two-thirds of the way along the walk. It is one of the most unspoilt of Chiltern villages, acquired by the NT (like many other properties in the area) in 1956 under the will of Mr E E Cook*

Follow the boundary wall as it turns left, then join and climb a gravel track. Where the wall turns left again, leave this gravel track and continue on a steeply-climbing woodland track, soon to rejoin the gravel track farther up the hill. Shortly after cottages on your right at the top of the climb, keep straight ahead on a grass path to enter Naphill Common. After 150y take a right fork; after another 300y ignore a right fork; 100y farther take the right fork and keep right yet again at the next fork to reach, after a small depression, a path junction adjacent to the corner of a field. Go ahead for another 20y, take a left fork away from the field and eventually you arrive among properties on the far side of the common. Turn right here along the edge of the common, first on a grass path and then a tarmac track.

After Woodbine Cottages, the last property on the left, continue on the common and then, just after the next property appears to your left, turn left along a tarmac road, Hunts Hill Lane. At the road junction

△ *Parish Church of St Botolph, Bradenham. Like many churches and other buildings in the Chilterns the flints for the facing were probably collected locally, since in some areas the chalk of the hills is replaced by mixed 'chalk-with-flints'. Quarrying is often unnecessary*

▷ *The golden-browns and russets of autumn shade the path near the turning to Bradenham Hill Farm*

ahead, immediately after the property Burnhams, go right on to a fenced gravel track running along the top of the ridge. After a stile at the end of the track, keep straight on along the edge of a long field with a hedge to the right. Near the far end of this field, go ahead over a stile to follow a gently descending woodland path to Hughenden Manor NT shop and Information Centre. Turn left here, walk down the road and return to the church at the start.

Hailes Abbey

A two-part ramble through Cotswold fields and villages and along the steep scarp north-east of Cheltenham. Two NT properties are visited: the Cistercian ruins of Hailes Abbey, and the practically untouched Tudor Snowshill Manor. Parts of the route are along the Cotswold Way.

These two linked walks form the two loops of a figure-eight. One extends 10m to the north-east of Hailes Abbey, via Stanway, Stanton, Shenberrow Camp, Snowshill Manor and Beckbury Camp; the other of 5m is to the south-west of the abbey via Winchcombe, Sudeley Castle and St Kenelm's Well. The full walk of

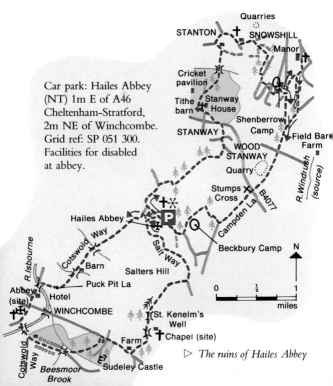

Car park: Hailes Abbey (NT) 1m E of A46 Cheltenham-Stratford, 2m NE of Winchcombe. Grid ref: SP 051 300. Facilities for disabled at abbey.

Quarries
STANTON
SNOWSHILL
Manor
Cricket pavilion
Stanway House
Tithe barn
STANWAY
Shenberrow Camp
Field Barn Farm
WOOD STANWAY
Quarry
R. Windrush (source)
Stumps Cross
Hailes Abbey
Cotswold Way
Salt Way
Campden La. B4077
Beckbury Camp
N
Barn
Salters Hill
R. Isbourne
Puck Pit La.
0   ½   1
miles
Abbey (site)
Hotel
WINCHCOMBE
St. Kenelm's Well
Farm
Chapel (site)
Cotswold Way
Beesmoor Brook
Sudeley Castle

▷ *The ruins of Hailes Abbey*

15m, crossing from one loop to the other at Hailes Abbey, is for experienced walkers with a day to spare. Parts of the scarp are steep and can be muddy, so do not underestimate your time: allow five hours for the 10m loop and $2\frac{1}{2}$ hours for the 5m one, plus time for visits, rests and exploration.

The small cluster of ruins at Hailes forms a striking picture, rising in lonely majesty from the flat green surroundings under the hanging wooded slopes. On a sunny day particularly, Hailes is homely, peaceful and very lovely. The abbey was a Cistercian house founded in 1246 by Richard, Earl of Cornwall, brother of Henry III, who gave the manor to him. The NT owns and protects the ruins, cottages, $19\frac{1}{2}$a of meadow and a museum of abbey relics, under the guardianship of the Department of the Environment.

The north-eastern loop (10m) of the walk, via Snowshill, commences past the equally old and beautiful church, which has some recently uncovered wall paintings, for about 300y down the lane to a footpath signposted *Wood Stanway*. The path follows a farm track at first, then headlands and open fields with fairly obvious stiles and gates and some waymarking.

▷ *Stanway Church, with the great house just visible to the rear*
▷ ▷ *Stanton with its village cross, the houses showing many hues of Cotswold stone. This pretty and compact village was developed under the eagle eye of architect Sir Philip Stott*
▽ *Cricket pavilion, Stanway*

The last field gate at Wood Stanway opens on to a pleasant street of cottages. Turn left at the first junction and right at the next, and immediately left again before the first dwelling. The route now joins the Cotswold Way long-distance footpath and is easily followed with its characteristic waymarks (white spots and yellow arrows) and obvious stiles ahead to the B4077 road at Stanway. This road was once the original 'Stoneway' which went straight up the scarp and on to Moreton-in-Marsh and Stow-on-the-Wold.

Turn left on the road for a few yards, then take the stile on the right to emerge in the village outside Stanway House and Church. The house was built in the reign of James I by Traceys of Toddington, and the gate-house is attributed to Inigo Jones. The house has a

remarkable great west window extending from ground to eaves and divided into 60 panes. In the grounds is a fine tithe barn which can be glimpsed from the road.

A few yards along the road you follow the finger-post on the right across pleasant sheep pasture and through avenues of fine trees. The way is indicated at intervals by marker posts and after the initial rise up the slope, crossing a stile and bearing left, you can enjoy a level walk with splendid views to Dumbleton and Bredon Hill (walk 11). The path goes through a gateway, over a footbridge, then over three stiles to Chestnut Farm, where a left turn gives access to Stanton village street.

More compact and pretty than Stanway, Stanton is almost too much of a model village where nothing is out of place. This is the influence of architect Sir Phillip Stott, who lived at Stanton Court from 1906 to 1937 and restored many of the cottages as well as dictating the harmonious orderliness which still prevails. Walk on past the church and cross, and follow the village street uphill, ignoring the Cotswold Way signs to the right — you are now leaving its route. As the slope steepens you come to the Mount Inn. Immediately behind the pub, and sometimes concealed in the foliage, the route takes an attractive shaded track leading up the scarp to old quarries.

△ *The track leading up the scarp from Stanton to the old quarries*
▷ *Looking south-west from Shenberrow Camp, towards Oxenton Hill*
▷ ▽ *Walking the Cotswold Way near Shenberrow Camp*

As the track levels out at the top, pass through two gates in succession. After the latter, neither deviate to the tracks left and right nor go downhill. Your line is straight across the open hillside, keeping on the same contour to the edge of the wood ahead. On reaching the woodland climb the slope directly in front. Overgrowth, broken drains and a tumbledown building tend to obstruct the way, but keeping slightly left, join a path and turn right behind the ruin to follow the glade uphill.

After 50y you are confronted by a pair of old stone gateposts. Do not pass through, but keep to the beech woods on the left of the old wire fence. Follow this fence until a dry-stone wall is reached; do not be tempted across the wire fence here, to a hunting gate, but turn sharp left up the slope to emerge on a track and then turn right through the gateway. Immediately turn off the track at 45 degrees, up the slope towards a group of trees. At the top of the slope cross the hairpin bend of a track in a hollow and then keep uphill, following the fence around Shenberrow hill fort.

Pass through the field gate on the left and rejoin the Cotswold Way for 100y to the bridleway fingerpost indicating a route around the farm buildings. The track passes between the barns and after the second it

turns sharp left to the skyline to meet an old stone road. (To avoid Snowshill and cut 2m from this walk turn right here to pick up the homeward leg.)

Turn left and in a few yards, immediately after the field boundary on the right, turn off the track on a line to Snowshill which is visible north-east across the valley. Although these fields are often cereal crops the path is usually well trodden. Cross a double stile and on the same line cross a further field to join the lane into the village. (For later reference, note the bridleway a few yards down the lane on the right.)

Snowshill is a beautiful village hidden away in this fold of the hills, at the head of a valley on the escarpment. Snowshill Manor (NT, 22½a) is a wonderfully preserved Tudor house with terraced gardens and collections of toys, musical instruments and tools of bygone ages.

Leave the village by the route you arrived on, as far as the bridleway noted above – which is now on your left. Go along it and past the farm building turn left and pass through a gateway to keep the dilapidated wall to your right. At the corner of the field join the old road which borders the wood for almost 1m ahead. At the isolated crossroad in the woods, keep straight ahead on the better-maintained, but still unclassified, road. Across the valley to the left is Field Barn Farm, source of the River Windrush.

The tree-lined road crosses the busy B4077 road to Stow-on-the-Wold at Stumps Cross, the remains of which are seen against the wall. You now rejoin the Cotswold Way and follow the bridleway track (Campden Lane) for ½m to a coppice where you turn right on to a further track. At the corner of the coppice pass through a gate on the left. The path follows the field boundary to the right, down to another coppice and then along the edge of the escarpment to Beckbury Camp, where Thomas Cromwell is reputed to have watched the destruction of Hailes Abbey. Descend the steep defensive bank of the camp and follow the Cotswold Way to the left, over two stiles to the old stone track which leads down through woods and back to Hailes Abbey.

The 5m south-western loop, via Winchcombe, now awaits those with enough stamina – or those who preferred not to visit Snowshill. From Hailes Abbey car park cross the road and take the Cotswold Way long-distance footpath across meadowland to a field gate. The short lane beyond leads to the old Salt Way, along which you return at the end of this walk. At the junction turn right, and after 100y follow the Cotswold Way along the bridlepath to the left. You will be on the Way as far as Winchcombe.

The track eventually turns right into cereal fields and becomes a sunken lane. After a short distance the path leaves the headland and cuts diagonally across to a

△ *Snowshill graveyard and Church. Note the lichen-covered stonework; lichens, primitive mixtures of algae and fungi, grow well in clean country air and 'marker' species are used to indicate degree of pollution*

△ *One of the many items collected at Snowshill Manor by its former owner Charles Wade. This NT property is worth a visit on account of its contents*
▷ *Stumps Cross, on the return*

stile (aim for the white target across the field). Shortly after is a gate; all this section is well waymarked. A faint track is discernible up the meadows ahead and as you breast the rise look for the views ahead of Winchcombe and St Peter's Church (famous for its gargoyles). This is the view thirteenth-century pilgrims would have had as they travelled between Hailes and the Benedictine Abbey of Winchcombe, said to have been founded by Kenulph, who was King of Mercia, in 798.

Our 'Pilgrims' Way' descends to Winchcombe by the quaintly named Puck Pit Lane. Walk along Hailes Street directly to the present-day George Hotel, which retains a Pilgrims' Gallery and original stonework of the Pilgrims' House founded by Richard Kidderminster, Abbot of Winchcombe, in the reign of Henry VII.

Although not preserved in the same manner as Chipping Campden, Winchcombe still exudes an atmosphere of antiquity rightly pertaining to a seat of kings and site of a once-great abbey. Remains of the abbey may be found in ornamental stonework of St Peter's and parts of the old houses in the attractive Gloucester Street. From the site of Kenulph's Abbey behind the wall of Abbey Terrace, descend Vineyard Street to the River Isbourne, shortly after which you diverge from the Cotswold Way and enter the

◁ *St Kenelm's Well, with Salters Hill rising in the background*
▷ *Gather the fruit of quince in early October*

grounds of Sudeley Castle park by the driveway.

The attractive tree-lined drive soon crosses an ornamental bridge over Beesmoor Brook. At the fingerpost take the path half-left, uphill to a hunting gate. Continue across the parkland in the same north-easterly line to the north lodge and a lane beyond. Turn right up the lane for $\frac{1}{4}$m to the attractive Cotswold stone buildings of Sudeley Hill Farm. From the fingerpost on the left follow the path diagonally up the steep pastures, over the stiles. Ahead now is the steep scarp slope of Salters Hill, where you regain the Salt Way. But before this, immediately in front are the site of St Kenelm's Well and Chapel.

The present well house was built by the third Lord Chandos, commemorating one of the three visits of Elizabeth I to Sudeley Castle.

From the stone access bridge below the well turn slightly left and cross the slope to a large ash tree and another access bridge. Your path from here makes directly for the obvious gate in the nick on the skyline, but the next slope is steep and sometimes obstructed by crops. From the gate on the skyline, the path goes straight across to the Salt Way on the crest of Salters Hill. This ancient road was mainly for pack animals carrying salt from 'Wiche' (Droitwich) to Lechlade, and thence by the Thames to London. The old way can be traced at such locations as Saltway Barn, Hinton-on-the-Green on the border with Worcestershire, and Saltway Farm near Coln St Denis. Domesday records salt refining at Toddington, the owner of which had seven salt pits at Wiche!

Turn left and follow the Salt Way down the hill, with Hailes Abbey now visible in the valley. Soon you turn right and retrace your steps back to the car park.

125

Useful information

The NT owns and protects well over 500,000a in England, Wales and Northern Ireland – about one per cent of the total land area. It is perhaps best known for its great country houses with their gardens and parks, but it was not for these that the organization came into existence in 1895. At that time the countryside itself and its smaller buildings were under threat, as towns and suburbs spread and places like the Lake District began to feel the full impact of the newly-mobile population. The first property acquired by the NT was a mere 4½a of clifftop at Dinas Oleu, near Barmouth in Gwynedd. Its first building was the historic but modest mid fourteenth-century Clergy House at Alfriston, East Sussex.

Today, the NT looks after 450m of the finest unspoilt coastline. It has 1,100 tenanted farms, and cares for one-quarter of the Lake District National Park and one-tenth of Snowdonia. There are huge tracts of NT land in the Peak District, South Wales, Dorset and Somerset, together with parts of the Malvern and Shropshire Hills and the Isle of Wight, and there are innumerable other NT properties scattered across the country.

When you are walking on NT land, look searchingly at your surroundings. Note how the woods, fields and copses are managed, how the paths are laid out and maintained, and how local features such as stiles, walls, barns and fences are looked after and renovated in keeping with the character of the countryside.

The NT's twin aims of access and conservation take time and money. The work is based on detailed management plans, often drawn up in consultation with bodies such as the Nature Conservancy Council, Countryside Commission, local county councils, and naturalists' and archaeological trusts. Walkers who gain pleasure from NT facilities can reciprocate by joining the NT – a charity that looks after large tracts of land and buildings for you, and for future generations, to enjoy for ever.

The National Trust, Central Office, 36 Queen
Anne's Gate, London SW1H 9AS;
phone 01-222 9251
Membership enquiries to: The National Trust,
Membership Department, PO Box 30, Beckenham,
Kent BR3 4TL; phone 01-650 7263
The National Trust, **Severn Regional Office**,
34–36 Church Street, Tewkesbury, Glos GL20 5SN;
phone Tewkesbury (0684) 292427
The National Trust, **Wessex Regional Office**,
Stourton, Warminster, Wilts BA12 6QD;
phone Bourton, Dorset (0747) 840224
The National Trust, **Thames & Chilterns
Regional Office**, Hughenden Manor, High
Wycombe, Bucks HP14 4LA;
phone High Wycombe (0494) 28051
**Gloucestershire Trust for Nature
Conservation**, Church House, Standish, Stonehouse,
Glos GL10 3EU
**Berks, Bucks and Oxon Naturalists' Trust
(BBONT)**, 3 Church Cowley Road, Rose Hill,
Oxford OX4 3JR
Cotswold Warden Service, County Planning
Department, Shire Hall, Gloucester GL1 2TN
Ramblers' Association, 1/5 Wandsworth Road,
London SW8 2LJ; phone 01-582 6878
Ordnance Survey, Romsey Road, Maybush,
Southampton SO9 4DH

Walkers are advised to plan their outings using
current NT information for details of opening days
and times and admission fees. Two invaluable
sources are *Properties of the National Trust* and the
Properties Open booklets relating to the region in
question.

Acknowledgements

Thanks are due to the following people for devising routes and writing walk accounts and features:
Tom Askwith, Ted Fryer, Peter Heaton, Jack Ibbott, Joan Kelland, Joyce Longhurst, Ivor Morris, Peter Nevell, Ron Seaborne, Cyril Shapter, Antony Spencer-Price, Geoffrey Stewart

Thanks also to the following for their help:
Kate Griffiths, Christopher Hall, Moira Morris, Roland Pomfret, Ramblers' Association, Roger Thomas

Illustrations by Andrew Aloof, Bob Bampton, Sandra Pond

Walk and locator map   Cooper West

Art work visualiser   Mike Trier

The publishers are grateful to the following companies and individuals:
Blacks of Holborn for camping equipment, Nikon UK Ltd for camera equipment, Fred and Kathy Gill, Format Publishing Service, Diana Greenman and Jane Parker